Brooke,

Always Remember...

¡Adelante!

Achieving "The American Dream"

by

María Jiménez Peña Tonkiss

María J. Tonkiss

DORRANCE PUBLISHING CO., INC.
PITTSBURGH, PENNSYLVANIA 15222

¡Adelante!
English Translation...Forward!

ISBN-10: 0-8059-7064-9
ISBN-13: 97800-8059-7064-7
Library of Congress Control Number: 2005931944
Printed in the United States of America

First Printing

For information or to order additional books, please write:
Dorrance Publishing Co., Inc.
701 Smithfield Street
Third Floor
Pittsburgh, Pennsylvania 15222
U.S.A.
1-800-788-7654
Or visit our website and online catalogue at www.dorrancebookstore.com

Acknowledgments

Thanks to my longtime friends, Zobeida Acevedo and Bess Carmichael, who encouraged me to write Mother's biography.

July 4th, 2003
A "Special Thanks" to Oprah with guests Maya Angelou, Billy Crystal and Sherman Alexi, who drove home the importance of connecting ourselves to the people of the past who sacrificed so much for us to have a better way of life. They motivated me to finish writing this biography.

My Remarkable Cheering Section

My "Granddaughter" Ashley Hope Oumano

Anita Allen, Rich Bonati, Dr. Robin Bliss, Betty Cartisano, Patty Chiusano, Pat Danvers, Consuela Domenick, Eileen Frappied, Gus (Bagel Lovers, Medford, NY), Irene Garbo, Joan Gould, Dr. Laura Hildebrant, Image Arts, Huntington, NY, Elaine Lawlor, Cristina Leal, Lynne McCormack, Marge Miller, Cliff Monges (my son-in-law), Paula Monges (my daughter), Jeffrey Monges (my grandson), Russell Monges (my grandson), Ryan Murphy, Zelda Nooger, Kathi Pagano, Kristine Pfister, Ele Ryder, Eric Scheer, Denise Scovanni, Michele Smith, Joan Sodero, U.S. Postal Workers, Middle Island, NY, Vanessa Stapleton, Elena Tonkiss (my daughter), Adele Worthington

The Breakfast Club—Bill Lynch, Art Pitschi, Jack Sexton, Gail Shafer, Phil Sheridan, Dan Visconti

My "Classmates"—The Round Table at Stony Brook University, New York

"The Joy of Writing" Leader—Hanna Marlens

"Memoir Writing" Leaders – Sheila Berber, Rhoda Selvin and Dorothy Shannon

Beta Psi Chapter—Pi State

The Delta Kappa Gamma Society International

Father Francis Pizzarelli—Hope House Ministries, Port Jefferson, New York

In Loving Memory of
Ramón Jiménez y Esperanza Peña Jiménez

It is very important that my children understand how I've reached this point in my life's journey. I want them to know me as a child. They should never take for granted what their grandparents had to overcome for them to have the privilege of living in this country.

Contents

*Each Chapter begins with a brief time capsule of world events to set the period.

> **1904:** The Supreme Court ruled that *Puerto Ricans* were not aliens and could enter the United States freely; however, the court stopped short of declaring them U.S. citizens.
>
> **1917:** *Puerto Ricans* were granted U.S. citizenship.

Introduction

1920: Two sixteen year olds from different countries came to the United States. They made a journey to an unknown land, not knowing how to speak, read or write English, each knowing inherently that it would be a better place to live. It would be a land of opportunity for them and their descendents as it had been in the past for others.

Ramón Jiménez, my father, entered the United States illegally. He made his way by bus, walking and hitchhiking from *Guadalajara, México* to New York.

At the same time that Father was traveling to New York, *Esperanza Peña*, my mother, was leaving *Vieques, Puerto Rico*. She took a ferry from *Vieques* (a small island located northeast of *Puerto Rico*) to *Fajardo*. From there she took a bus, walked and hitchhiked to the harbor in *Old San Juan* where she boarded a ship en route to New York.

I loved my father very much, but I know in my heart of hearts that I'm writing this for Mother. It is her story. She was an incredible woman who without any formal education achieved "The American Dream." I learned right from wrong, a strong work ethic, how to be a survivor, the importance of an education, and above all, *never* to give up on my hopes and dreams. This biography is a testimonial and a chronicle of an exceptional woman.

Gracias Mamá, hasta otro tiempo. (Thank you Mother, until another time.)
Cariños ... mi amor, (love, affection ... my love,)

María

Ramón Jiménez born in *Guadalajara, México*
(1904 – 1951)

Esperanza Peña born in *Vieques, Puerto Rico*
(1904 – 1984)

They were both sixteen years old when they started their journey to the
United States in 1920.

1924:

J. Edgar Hoover was given the job of FBI director.
The Statue of Liberty was declared a national monument.

Mamá

Chapter I

"*¡Rápido! ¡Rápido! ¡Rápido, Esperanza! ¡Se van a escapar!*" (Hurry! Hurry! Hurry, *Esperanza*! They're going to escape!)

Life could be perilous in *Vieques*, a small island located northeast of *Puerto Rico's* main island. She was twelve years old when one of the men of the household asked her to go out with him on a small boat. When they were far from shore, he lit explosives that he was carrying and threw them into the water. The explosion rocked the boat and stunned whatever fish were in the area so that they bobbed up to the surface, momentarily motionless. It was then that she realized why she had been asked to go along. While the man rowed as fast as he could, her job was to scoop up as many fish as possible before they recovered and swam away. She had been drawn into an illegal way of fishing.

> 1924: The year Mother was married. She was twenty years old. On the back of the photo she wrote, "*Esta foto es antes de tener hijos cuando se usaba la ropa larga.*" (This photo is before having children when clothes were worn longer)

1

(February 25, 2004—*Vieques*—The house is over one hundred years old and is the style of home that Mother lived in. The photo shows how the homes were built about two or three feet above the ground.)

This became one of the chores that she hated and feared the most. She knew that it was dangerous: many people had been badly injured while handling the explosives.

Mother rarely spoke about her childhood in *Vieques, Puerto Rico* and how she came to Island Park, New York. I just remember being told bits and pieces growing up. I've put them together to the best of my recollection.

My grandmother died giving birth to her, and my grandfather died a few years later in a boating accident. An orphan at nine years old, she was sent to live with a family as a mother's helper. The reality was, she was their maid. For one so young, she had tremendous responsibilities and as a consequence never had a childhood.

The homes in *Vieques* were built on cement blocks, about two or three feet above the ground. The children often played in the crawl space under the house. They built a tiny play kitchen with a small fire to cook.

On one occasion the children heated a small pan of fat to fry a mixture of flour and water. Mother was playing with the little girl of the house that she took care of (they were both ten years old). Mother put the fork in the fat, it became very hot and suddenly on an impulse she stuck it in the little girl's hand. It sizzled when it hit the skin and the little girl started to scream and cry. When Mother told me the story I was taken aback, because it was the antithesis of what she was all about. I never knew her to be mean in any way. She was a nurturing person and would open her arms in kindness to everyone. I think she was suddenly jealous of what that little girl had … a mother, a father and a home. She had no one, she was just a servant.

Many years later when she told me the story, she said regretfully, "*María, me da muchísima pena que hice eso!*" (Maria, I'm so sorry I did that!)

Life was hard in *Vieques* and family members often physically abused her. If she didn't do what she was told to do fast enough, or, if for some reason it wasn't done the way they wanted, she was hit on the head and body. It could be with pots, pans, wooden spoons, or whatever was handy. Years later she showed me the permanent lumps on her head from having been hit repeatedly.

Mother was sixteen years old when a woman came to visit from Island Park, New York. She was a friend of the family for whom Mother worked. The woman from Island Park took a liking to Mother and told her that if she came to the States she could start a new life. She could earn money by caring for her children. The opportunity seemed

1920's—Mother when she first arrived in Island Park

like a dream come true. The woman left and later sent just enough money for the boat fare.

At the age of sixteen, an orphan and alone, Mother took a ferry from *Vieques* to *Fajardo*. She walked part of the way and took a bus from *Fajardo* to the harbor in *Old San Juan* where she boarded a ship that took her to New York.

The opportunity did not turn out to be a dream come true. On the contrary it became a nightmare. The abuse continued. Her work was not as pleasant as it had been described to her in *Vieques*. As soon as she arrived in Island Park she was put to work in a laundry in Long Beach. The woman kept her salary from the laundry and the only money she was given was bus fare to go to work.

Mother secretly started putting money aside. She walked to and from work and hid her bus fare. The woman found the money, took it and told Mother, "*Bueno, Esperanza como te gusta caminar tanto no necesitas dinero para la guagua! Así es que puedes caminar!*" (Well, *Esperanza*, since you like walking so much you don't need money for the bus! So, you can walk!)

¿Dios mío, qué voy a hacer con mi vida? (My God, what am I going to do with my life?)

There were very few Spanish speaking people at the laundry. She didn't know anyone in Island Park and even if she did, she was unable to communicate because she didn't speak English. She never had a day off to explore her options. There was no alternative but to continue her miserable existence until hopefully, something changed.

For now, she was trapped.

1910—1920s *The Mexican Revolution. The decade is one of the most turbulent periods in Mexican History. It was a nation in flux where lawlessness prevailed.*

1927: *Charles A. Lindbergh completed the first solo flight across the Atlantic. The era of talking pictures arrived with "The Jazz Singer."*

Papá

Chapter II

It was a beautiful, tranquil day. *Ramón* was playing in the fields near the house where he had grown up. Without warning the day became a nightmare that would haunt him throughout his life. Hidden by the shrubs and tall grass he watched helplessly as he saw a band of renegade outlaws on horseback descend upon his home. The sounds became one loud horrific roar from hell! The restless horses, the men yelling commands, his father fighting, his mother's screams ... to no avail.

He watched as if he were in a trance. The bandits tied his parents to a tree and executed them. The shots rang in his ears. As suddenly as they had come, they were gone and it was deadly quiet.

¡Dios mío! ¡Dios mío! ¡Dios mío!

As long as he lived he had no memory of how long he stayed in the field.

1920—*Ramón Jiménez*, my father, saw his parents murdered ... he was sixteen years old. Escaping was his priority; there was no future

This oval portrait 18" x 24" was Father's wedding gift to Mother.

for him in *México*. He rarely spoke about his youth but the incident affected his life.

At the same time that Mother was making her way to Island Park, Father was coming into this country via another route. He made his way by bus, walking and hitch-hiking from *Guadalajara, México* to Texas. He had entered the country illegally and became friendly with Mr. and Mrs. Piza in Texas. I have no idea how they met.

Mr. and Mrs. Piza were very wealthy and took a liking to this personable young man. They hired him as a cabin boy and he traveled with them extensively. The Piza's didn't have children and they adored Father. He was the son they never had.

Eventually he came with them to Atlantic Beach, New York which at the time was a wealthy summer community established by Sephardic Jews. The architecture was decidedly Spanish and the homes had the Spanish tile roofs reminiscent of Spain. Father was living with Mr. and Mrs. Piza and working for them as a handyman doing odd jobs.

Mr. Piza had a lot of contacts and he introduced Father to his friends and associates. Father started by painting houses. Later, when the owners moved south during the winter months, he repaired and maintained the expensive homes and the Atlantic Beach Club. Father had a reputation for being honest and a hard worker. It was easy for him to speak to the owners, for the most part Sephardic Jews who were fluent in Spanish. Not having a language barrier worked in his favor and his business started doing very well.

Mrs. Piza delighted in telling a particular story about my father when he had first come to live with them. His English was limited and he was busy painting one of the rooms in the Piza's house. Suddenly Father started yelling, "*¡Señora! ¡Señora!*" She ran to see what the problem was. He said, "*¡Señora*, the dog shit!" With this she went to get a pan and brush to clean up the mess. She came back and looked but couldn't find anything.

"*Ramón*, where is the shit?"

He looked at her and then at the pan and brush. Frustrated, he shook his head, "No *Señora*, not that kind of shit. This kind, and with that he pursed his lips and made the sound of a fart." Mrs. Piza couldn't stop laughing.

In the spring of 1924, he met a friend who was employed in the laundry where Mother worked. By chance his friend introduced my parents. They took a liking to each other and started meeting secretly.

Mother, of course was delighted to meet this good-looking young man and most important, he spoke Spanish. They were the same age and he was immediately attracted to this pretty, Hispanic woman. They fell in love. Mother's dream of starting a new life seemed to be coming true.

1925—*Ramón Jiménez* and *Esperanza Peña* were married and those were the good years. They were young, very much in love and together had the opportunity of realizing "The American Dream." Mother said the happiest day of her life was telling the woman who had been so abusive to her that she was leaving her employ to get married.

Growing up I realized that Father's schooling was limited in *México*. He couldn't read or write Spanish or English. Being illiterate was a problem that he seemed able to circumvent to a point with his winning personality. He was a charmer. I remember seeing cans of house paint stacked neatly in the garage. On the outside of each can he had painted color swatches so that he knew what colors he had in stock.

As a teenager my father volunteered my babysitting services to a wealthy family in Atlantic Beach. It was time for lunch and I was asked to join the family. The dining room was set up as if a formal dinner was about to be served.

They had a full time cook, butler, and maid. We sat at the table and as the maid was serving us the delicious meal that the cook had prepared, the butler came in with a white sheet and draped it over one of the plush, velvet upholstered dining room chairs. It was to the right of the head of the household.

Why did the butler cover the chair with a white sheet?

A few minutes later my question was answered. Father walked in laughing and chatting as if he were at home. "*¿Qué tal? ¿Y cómo está el patrón?*" (How's everything? And how's the boss doing?)

He was wearing his work clothes and a painter's cap. He went into the kitchen, joked with the cook, scrubbed his hands and came back to the dining room. He promptly took off his cap and put it on the back of the chair as he sat down on the draped chair feeling perfectly at ease. As we ate he used a napkin to hold his bread, as he had paint on his hands and he didn't want it to touch his food. I sensed that he stopped by often.

Everyone clearly liked and enjoyed Father's company … it was a wonderful day.

1920–1930s Long Beach bridge. To the left was the laundry where my parents met.

1920s—Father

1929—Father with his first car.

Island Park

Chapter III

My parents had come a long way from *Guadalajara, México* and *Vieques, Puerto Rico.*

Father continued working in Atlantic Beach and Mother kept her job at the laundry. She had decided from the beginning of her marriage that they would never live in Spanish Harlem. She knew intuitively that her family would have a better quality of life in Island Park. In 1930, because of Mother's resolve and thriftiness, my parents were able to purchase a small house on Newport Road, Island Park, New York.

They owned their home, had money in the bank, a car and lots of friends. They were living "The American Dream."

Island Park is a one square mile island located between Oceanside and Long Beach. It was originally a summer community and is close enough to commute to Manhattan for the day. Former Republican Senator Alfonse "Tippie" D'Amato, a long time resident, is its only claim to fame. He is known on Long Island as "Senator Pothole" for his responsiveness to constituents' requests and the HUD scandal of the 1980s.

Originally the town was primarily a community of white, working class people who lived in neatly painted, unpretentious homes on small, well-tended lots. Many of the homes were summer bungalows, now converted to year-round use.

Island Park was a Christian town. There were a few Jewish families. My Jewish classmates were subjected to prejudice, especially at Easter time. I don't remember any Blacks living in Island Park. Looking back, I was never the object of prejudice. I'm sure that it was there but I wasn't aware of it until Father died.

Once a month my family made a special day trip to Spanish Harlem "*La Marqueta*" to buy Spanish groceries that were unavailable locally. Mother

1933—My parents' first home was on Newport Road, Island Park.

had to have her special seasonings, meat, fruit, and vegetables to cook her *Puerto Rican* specialties.

When my parents first moved into their home Mother wanted to start a family immediately but Father wanted to wait. Having been an orphan, she now wanted the family she never had. He on the other hand had a wife, a good business, a home, a car and lots of friends. They had company almost every weekend and he was having a great time enjoying the good life. He didn't want to be tied down with the responsibilities that came with having children.

Mother became pregnant and my father insisted she have an abortion. It was performed at home. She hemorrhaged so badly that her blood went through the mattress onto the floor. The abortionist couldn't stop the bleeding … she almost died.

It was at that moment that she started falling out of love with my father. What he had asked her to do and what she had allowed herself to do broke her heart. Later in life she would often talk about that first baby. It was a boy. The ache for that lost child never left her.

With a heavy heart Mother would say, "*Perdí mi alma y mi corazón.*" (I lost my soul and my heart.)

Mother persevered. She wanted a family, her very own family. She became pregnant again. This time she didn't tell my father and kept it a secret from him until it was too late to abort the unborn child. He was furious; she had deceived him and it caused a widening rift between them.

I was born July 2, 1934 in Long Beach Hospital, *Maria Jiménez Peña*. For whatever reason my father did a complete turnaround. He was ecstatic to have a child and I was the apple of his eye until the day he died. Happiness prevailed for a time … they were now a family.

A large portrait of my father, in an elegant oval frame was always displayed in a prominent place in my parents' bedroom. I thought it strange that they didn't have a wedding picture of both of them. It was Father's wedding gift to Mother. I never knew what she gave him. He was very much into being the "*Macho*" (the Man) of the house. He had a high opinion of himself, was outgoing, liked people, and loved to party. Father

I was one year old.

was happiest when we had a house full of company.

Mother on the other hand loved to take care of her family and home. I can still see her sweeping the porch and hear her singing softly, "*Mi Capullito De Alelí,*" her favorite song. She was at peace. She liked having company and entertaining but certainly not to the extent that my father did. She was a fabulous dancer and when she was in a party mood there was *no one* that could move their hips as seductively to the rhythm of Latin music as Mother.

Every Sunday she would get up early and cook a full course *Puerto Rican* dinner. Friends and neighbors knew that we ate Sunday dinner at 1:00 P.M. and they were welcome to join us. We never knew who would show up but we always had guests on Sundays. Everyone brought something for the dinner table: a bottle of wine, dessert, or flowers.

I have fond memories of growing up in Island Park. We were privileged to have the beach within walking distance from our home. The summers were wonderful. We went to the beach early in the morning and spent the entire day there. Very often Father joined us to go swimming.

Summers ended with a great Labor Day celebration at the beach. One of the events was the mile swimming race. It started at the Island Park Canal and ended at the Island Park Beach. The canal had a series of small bridges connecting Island Park to Harbor Isle. When I was in the race my father would jump in his truck and drive from one bridge to the next. He would be on the bridge as I swam under it, yelling and encouraging me!

I was two years old.

1941—Father/Ray/Me—Island Park Beach

Mother/Father in the backyard.

"*¡Vaya, María! ¡Vaya, María!*" "Go, María! Go, María!"

Of course I was embarrassed, I so wanted to be American but he meant well and we always had a wonderful time.

It was very important for me to fit in and be an American, at the same time holding on to my Hispanic identity. All through my school years I was the only Hispanic in my class. There was never any question that learning English was a priority in our family. When we were at home we spoke Spanish. The moment we stepped outside, we spoke English. When I started school my English was pretty good and I have always been fluent in Spanish.

On the other hand my brother was adamant ... he refused to speak Spanish. If my parents spoke to him in Spanish, especially if they spoke to him in front of his friends, he would throw a tantrum. Today he regrets that he only knows a few words of Spanish. He realizes how his business could really prosper if he were bilingual.

Summers Were Wonderful!

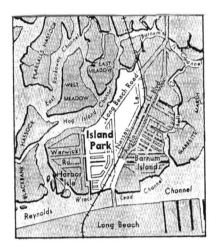

Island Park, New York

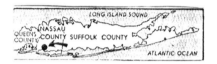

1931–1932 Our house and car on Newport Road, Island Park. Quite an accomplishment!

Summers Were Wonderful!

Island Park ...

Located between Oceanside and Long Beach.

Newport Road ... our first house.

Marina Road ... our second house.

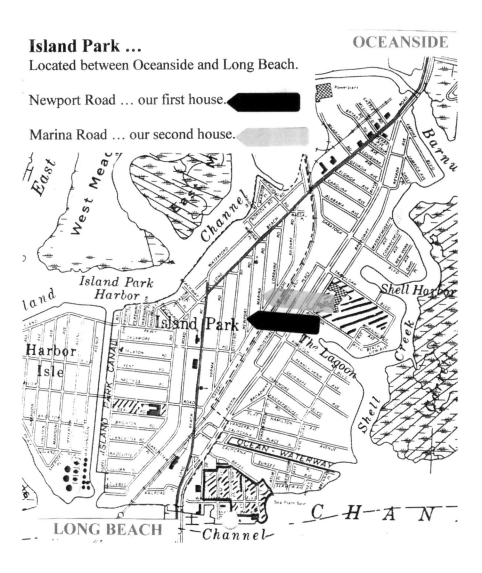

Summers Were Wonderful!

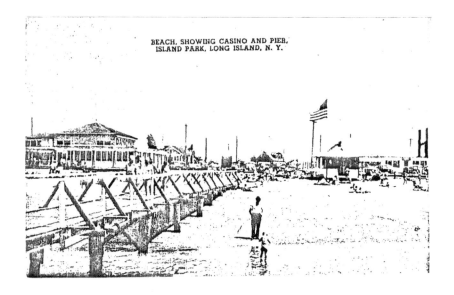

BEACH, SHOWING CASINO AND PIER,
ISLAND PARK, LONG ISLAND, N. Y.

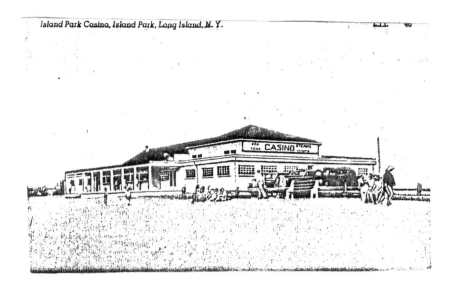

Island Park Casino, Island Park, Long Island, N. Y.

Summers Were Wonderful!

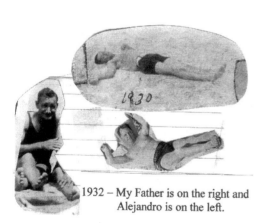

1932 – My Father is on the right and Alejandro is on the left.

1932 – Mother 2nd row, 3rd person from left with friends.

Summers Were Wonderful!

1938 – I was four years old.

1931 – A friend, my father, and Mother on the right.

1939 – 1940
Left… a friend and me.
Right…
Friends.

Summers Were Wonderful!

1941 – At the Island Park Beach with friends, I'm 1st, 2nd row, left side.

1951 – Left, I'm in front of our house. Center, I'm holding a friend's baby in front of our house. Right, I'm at the beach.

The Depression

Chapter IV

This photo was taken during the Depression. The men were clearing Main Street, Island Park, New York after a snowstorm. My father is the second man from the right, wearing the plaid coat.

There was no work. My father worked for the W.P.A. (Works Projects Administration), also known as "We Poke Along." Most of the parkways that were built in the 1930s on Long Island were constructed by the labor force of the W.P.A.

Franklin D. Roosevelt established the W.P.A. in 1935. Some 3.5 million jobless Americans worked on roads, parks, and buildings. The W.P.A. became the largest employer of labor in American history. The salaries paid provided a decent living and most important, self-respect was maintained for millions of Americans.

The Laurel Movie Theatre

Chapter V

Going to the movies was a special treat ... television didn't come into our lives until much later. The Laurel movie theatre was located in Long Beach and was a forty minute drive from Island Park.

Two movies stand out: 1938—I was four years old, Mother and Father had taken me to the theatre to see *Snow White and The Seven Dwarfs*. It was sold out and the only seats left were way up front. Being so close to the screen made it all the more vivid ... especially the scene with the witch standing on the mountain with thunder and lightning crashing, and the rain and the wind swirling around her as she cackled. Scary stuff for a child but it was okay because I was sitting between Mother and Father and I felt safe.

1946—The circumstances were radically different.

The movie was *The Jolson Story* starring Larry Parks and Evelyn Keyes. It was a very cold, wintry, Saturday evening. Mother, Ray and I were chilled

21

Veinte y Uno

to the bone waiting for the bus on the steps of the neighborhood deli. We took the bus from Island Park to the Long Beach railroad station. From there it was a good fifteen minute walk to the movies.

Father was drinking more and was always looking for an argument. Mother had taken us to the movies to escape the turmoil for at least an evening.

However, it was not to be. We were watching the show when about half way through the movie Father walked into the theatre looking for us. She saw him first and signaled us to be quiet and not to take notice of him. He had come into a dark theatre and couldn't see us.

Not to be deterred he stopped in the middle of the aisle and started yelling,

"¡Esperanza! ¡María! ¡Ramón!"

He kept calling us, each time louder. Mother, humiliated, finally gave up and we left with him.

We never saw the end of the movie. We got in his car and they fought all the way home. There was no getting away from it. They were always arguing about the same thing … his increasing episodes of drinking, gambling, womanizing, and partying.

They were miserable and Ray and I in turn were just as miserable. There was no peace.

The Typewriter

Chapter VI

1939—My first day of school.

That morning I was up, dressed and ready to go to school an hour before we had to leave. I was so excited! Mother and I had carefully chosen my outfit the night before.

"*¿María, te gusta este vestido?*" (*María*, do you like this dress?)

Every detail: dress, sweater, socks, shoes, and of course the ribbons in my hair had to match.

Father had bought me a beautiful school bag and a Mickey Mouse watch to complete the outfit.

He was laughing when he said, "*¡Esta noche hay otro regalo **especial**!*" (Tonight there's another *special* gift!)

That afternoon Father and I drove to Atlantic Beach to visit Mr. and Mrs. Piza, his benefactors. He was proud of me and it was very important that they saw me the first day of school. Mr. Piza took the photo of me standing on their front stoop.

All the while I kept thinking, *What's the special gift?*

We returned home and on the table, beautifully gift wrapped, was the present he had promised—a foreign language typewriter. I was delighted and immediately started typing, pecking style, copying words from books.

Of course, Father had a plan. Within a week I was typing his bills. I copied the client's names from their business cards and he told me the dollar amounts to fill in. I was five years old and doing my father's billing.

He proudly announced, "*¡Eres mi secretaria!*" (You're my secretary!)

To make it official, he paid me one dollar for every bill I wrote. At a very young age I felt important.

I was in the eighth grade when Mother told me she was opening a checking account in the local bank.

"*Pero, hay un problema. María, necesito tu ayuda.* (But, there's a problem. *María*, I need your help.) I understand how to write checks but I can't spell the numbers. Would you type a chart listing the numbers and the spelling next to each number?"

I was pleased. Not only was I doing my father's billing but I was learning how to write checks! I prepared a detailed chart with the numbers written numerically followed by the spelling. She kept it with her checkbook and referred to it for years.

Puerto Rico

Chapter VII

1939 - Ray/Me

The negative effects of the Depression of the 1930s were subsiding. The forties were fast approaching. World War II was on the horizon and the nation started to prosper.

My father worked as a laborer for the W.P.A. (Works Projects Administration), and did side jobs. Mother continued working in the laundry in Long Beach. She often walked along the railroad tracks and picked up bits of coal that had fallen from the trains to be used in our coal stove at home. Although many people lost everything, my family didn't really suffer during the Depression. My parents were able to hold on to their home.

1939 – Father in front
of the Piza's
home in
Atlantic Beach.

1939 - NY harbor.
I'm standing in the
front, Mother (with hat)
is in the back and neighbors
who had come to wish us
Bon Voyage!

I was seven years old and Ray was two years old when Mother decided to return to *Puerto Rico*. My father's drinking had accelerated, he was gambling heavily, and they were constantly arguing. She had every intention of staying.

I was excited; we were going on an ocean voyage! Mother, on the other hand, was nervous and Ray was oblivious to what was happening around him. He was just a happy toddler loving all the activity in preparation for the trip.

Mother had good reason to be concerned. It was scary in those days; German submarines had been sighted in the shipping lanes on our route. The captain of the ship informed the passengers not to throw anything overboard, fearing that a U-boat might pick up our trail and sink us.

The three of us watched the sunrise as our ship entered the port of *Old San Juan* and approached the docking area. The glow of the tropical sun gave the harbor the appearance of a beautiful picture postcard.

She had left *Puerto Rico* nineteen years ago, alone, and was returning with her children. Would her dear childhood friends, *Carmen*, *Candita*, and *María*, recognize her?

Suddenly, *"¡Esperanza! ¡Esperanza!"*

There they were just as she remembered them. Waving, laughing and crying at the same time, unable to contain their joy in seeing their friend.

Ray and I were more interested in watching the children who were diving from the pier into the water. It was quite steep and we were fascinated. They were diving for coins that passengers were tossing from the ship.

We stayed with *Carmen* in *Río Piedras* near the University of *Puerto Rico*. I have happy memories of living in that pretty little house. However, at Christmas time I was very disappointed that we celebrated *Día de los Reyes* (Three Kings Day) and not a visit from Santa Claus. Who ever heard of putting hay in a box for the Three Wise Men's camels? I wanted to leave cookies and milk for Santa. To make it worse *Día de los Reyes* is celebrated January 6th ... twelve days after Christmas! My favorite gift was a little red umbrella with a Scotty dog on the handle. I cherished it and took it everywhere I went ... rain or shine!

Ray and I especially enjoyed the weekends spent at *Fajardo* beach. We loved swimming, playing and picnicking. The ferry to *Vieques* was nearby but

1940 – Ray/Me
Fajardo
beach.

we never made the boat trip to that small island. There was nothing there for Mother but painful memories of her childhood that were best left alone.

Mother never told me the reason for a very strange visit and I didn't ask her any questions. I was just happy being with Mother.

"*El Fanguito*" (*Fanguito*: little mud) was a neighborhood comprised of wooden houses that were built on stilts above golden brownish clay with water running through in little rivulets. The plank sidewalks were also on stilts, giving the neighborhood a strange eerie appearance. The hot tropical heat and the terrible stench seemed to permeate everything. Mother and I stayed for about an hour. We never returned

The time spent in the beautiful mountains of *Puerto Rico* is a treasured memory. As we drove to *Candita's* home for a visit we could see the men hard at work in the sugar cane fields. Sometimes we would stop and as a treat the men would give us a piece of sugar cane to suck on like candy. It is delicious! To prepare it they would hold a stalk of sugar cane in their hand and with a *machete* they would hack off the outside part until there was just the sweet center left.

One day when no adults were around, I took it upon myself to take a *machete* and whittle down the sugar cane as I had seen the men do so often. It was a big mistake. With the first swing of the *machete* (holding the sugar cane in my left hand, *machete* in my right) I almost cut my thumb off.

It was gushing blood, the pain was excruciating, and the children started screaming and running to get Mother.

"*¡Doña Esperanza! ¡Doña Esperanza!*"

I clamped my thumb firmly between the other fingers and put my hand behind my back. Mother came to see what the commotion was all about. I was more afraid of her being angry than losing my thumb. She immediately saw what had happened, took me in her arms and rushed me to the doctor. Afterwards, she gave me a piece of sugar cane and told me the next time I should be patient and ask an adult for help.

"*¡María eres muy chiquita, no puedes usar un machete!*" (*María* you're too small, you can't use a *machete*!)

Candita's husband worked for a *patrón*, a wealthy man who owned a lot of land, cattle, pigs, and poultry. This boss parceled out land, and the people planted crops. At the end of the season they would have to pay him a percentage of what they earned. *Puerto Rican* sharecropping!

It was very important to *Candita* to make a special meal to celebrate Mother's visit. However, it had been a bad year and there wasn't much money in her budget for the luxury of having meat at the dinner table. She would have to improvise to get some chickens for dinner.

She closed all the windows and doors in the neat, small wooden house with the exception of the front door. Next, someone made a trail of kernels of corn from the middle of the room out to the walkway. This attracted the chickens and they started scurrying into the house eating the corn as fast as they could. As soon as there were three chickens in the house the door was slammed shut and the chickens were trapped. What squealing and yelling!

"*¡Rápido, rápido ... se van a escapar!*" (**Hurry, hurry ... they're going to escape!**)

Feathers flew in all directions! So much chaos until the chickens were caught and killed. There was great concern about getting rid of the feathers ... the evidence of what had happened to the *patrón's* chickens. I stood there not believing the scenario that had just unfolded so quickly and methodically.

All through dinner I was terrified that the *patrón* was going to burst in and yell, "*¿Dónde están mis gallinas? ¡Ladrones, robaron mis gallinas!*" (**Where are my chickens? Thieves, you stole my chickens!**)

Mother, Ray and I returned to *Río Piedras*. We had lived in *Puerto Rico* for almost a year. During that time Father kept making phone calls and writing letters imploring Mother to come home. He never let up ... insisting that he couldn't live without his family and assuring her that he had changed for the better. He had been working very hard on a special surprise for her.

"*¡Esperanza, mi amor ... te va a encantar!*" (Esperanza, my love ... you're going to love it!)

Ray and I missed Father and we wanted to go home. We kept asking, "*¿Cuándo vamos a ver a Papá?*" (When are we going to see Father?)

Mother finally gave in. One evening I overheard her tell *Carmen*, "*¡Tengo que regresar!*" (I have to return.)

I was delighted to hear her tell her friend that we were going home. The long visit made her realize that there was nothing for her in her native *Puerto Rico* and that she would have a better life for her children and herself with my father.

1940 –
Friends/Me
The University
Of Puerto Rico,
Río Piedras.

Puerto Rico

1940 – 1941
Ray, (left)
Friends/Me at the University of Puerto Rico Campus. (right)

Puerto Rico

1940 – Me with friend – Rio Piedras

1940 - My Brother, Ray on the porch – Río Piedras

1940 – My brother in the front. I'm holding the doll with friends, Rio Piedras.

Father's Stairs

Chapter VIII

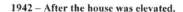

1933 – The original house.

1942 – After the house was elevated.

Mother stood against the ship's railing taking a last look at *Puerto Rico* as we sailed out of *San Juan* harbor toward New York. She had taken Ray and me to *Puerto Rico* intending to divorce our father and start a new life.

He had been relentless, calling her on the phone day after day imploring her to come home and swearing by *La Virgen De Guadalupe* that he had changed for the better. He repeatedly expressed his love for her and his children. He cried that he couldn't live without his family. She was going back to him but had she made the right decision?

"*No sé, no sé.*" (I don't know, I don't know.) So many unanswered questions as the ship made its way back to New York.

When we arrived he was standing at the dock crying, waving, and throwing kisses. We had been gone for almost a year and he was ecstatic to have his family back. We hugged, kissed, and talked all the way home about all of the things we had seen and done in *Puerto Rico*. He in turn told us he had been very busy working on a special surprise for Mother. He was desperately trying to impress her.

As we approached our house Mother saw the surprise and exclaimed, **"¡Dios mío Ramón! ¿Qué demonio hiciste con las escaleras?"** (**My God, Ramón! What the hell did you do to the stairs?**

He had raised the house and converted it from a bungalow to two stories. The stairs were the first thing we saw, they were a disaster! He built them straight up to the second floor, solid cement with no railings.

From the very beginning Mother hated the stairs. They were so unsightly. In the winter when there was ice and snow it was treacherous going up and down. It was an ongoing argument between them until they finally moved to another house. She said they looked exactly like the flights of stairs going up to the subway platforms in New York City and she was right, they did.

Years later I realized that the staircase looked exactly like the steps of the Aztec temples in *México*. My father was always very proud of his work on the house. As a boy he had seen many Aztec temples. To duplicate the architecture of the steps going straight up to the top of the temple gave him a great feeling of accomplishment

Railings have been added, but the steps on the house basically remain the same. The people who now own the house some seventy-one years later don't know the controversy the stairs caused and that it reflects a past culture of *México*.

2004 – The house as it is today.

Education

Chapter IX

Education is not the filling of a pail, but the lighting of a fire. —William Butler Yeats

Growing up in *Puerto Rico* Mother never had a formal education but she could read and write Spanish. She taught herself to read English, spending hours going over comic books and figuring out what the words meant by looking at the pictures. During his lifetime Father never learned to read or write Spanish or English.

Mother always emphasized the importance of an education and would say, *"¡María, fíjate, no quieres limpiar casas!"* (*María*, look, you don't want to clean houses!)

or

"¡Una educación es tuya para siempre nadie te la puede quitar!" (An education is yours forever, no one can take it away from you!)

or

"¡Además, eres independiente!"

(Furthermore, you're independent!)

I learned at a very young age that if I was reading a book or doing school work, I didn't have to do chores. As a result the more I read the more I loved reading ... I was hooked! Despite the chaos at home I always applied myself and excelled in school.

Mother would say, *"¡Shhhh, María está estudiando!"* (Shhhh, *María* is studying!)

It was as if she'd waved a magic wand ... no one bothered me! I could escape the insanity for a while. I became an avid reader; the written word introduced me to fascinating people and transported me to far off places.

Life at home was miserable. Mother was the force that kept us focused and together as a family. Always with her spirit of, *"¡Adelante!"* (Forward!) she made us feel that we could get through any adversity as long as we persevered.

There were periods of laughter and joy but it was always short lived because of Father's drinking, gambling, and womanizing. The promises he had made convincing Mother to return from *Puerto Rico* were short lived. In the dark shadows there was always the insidious dysfunction and drama of the alcoholic, waiting to jump in at any moment and destroy the good times. We never knew what state of mind or mood he would be in when he came home.

My good fortune was that I had an absolutely incredible teacher in elementary school. Her name was Mrs. Shertenlieb and I adored her. Sometimes when I'm in a public place, I get a whiff of the perfume she used and it brings back wonderful memories of time spent with her.

Mrs. Shertenlieb was my *Special Angel*.

All through my school years I was the only Hispanic in my classes. In the 1940s there were no bilingual programs. Mrs. Shertenlieb tutored me in English and went a step further to make me feel special. Once a week she encouraged me to teach a Spanish lesson to the class. I was nine years old and felt so important! Mrs. Shertenlieb was that exceptional teacher who had the capacity to make a difference in a child's life.

Years later, I found this letter in the attic that Mother had saved:

May 12, 1943

Dear Mrs. Jiménez,

Today Mary taught us a Spanish lesson which we all enjoyed, especially her teacher.

For one so young, Mary has excellent qualities for leadership.

Perhaps some day she'll be teaching Spanish in one of our high schools. I do believe she would make an excellent teacher.

Sincerely,

Agnes Shertenlieb

My parents were honored when Mrs. Shertenlieb asked if I could spend time with her on the weekends. It became routine, Saturday morning she would come to my home and pick me up.

Mother would tell me, "*María, pórtate bien. Es un honor ir a la casa de tu maestra.*" (*María,* behave yourself. It's an honor to go to your teacher's home.)

Mrs. Shertenlieb and I talked, read and she showed me pictures of her husband. He had a great smile and was very handsome in his uniform. It was World War II and he was in the army fighting in Europe. We had lunch and waited for the mailman to deliver the mail. It was a good day if she got a letter from him. It meant that he was safe. I felt privileged when she shared his letters with me.

World War II was not like the war in Iraq.

2003—Iraq—There was instantaneous communication with the troops. CNN and all the other networks kept the world informed as events developed minute by minute.

1943—World War II– Weeks and months went by and you didn't know what was happening to your loved ones. It was the waiting and not knowing that was the toughest for the people at home.

Mr. Shertenlieb did come home safe from World War II. I continued my schooling and lost touch with Mrs. Shertenlieb. Years later I tried to locate her. At the time I was living in West Islip and was told that she had passed away the year before. She had lived in Bay Shore for years not too far from where I was living. She had never had children but I'm sure that in her years of teaching she motivated and touched many children's hearts. I'm a better human being for having had her as a teacher and wish I could have told her so in person.

I'm very fortunate to have had two strong women as role models in my life. If I hadn't had Mother and Mrs. Shertenlieb guiding me I might not have made the right choices. Each in their own special way instilled in me tremendous self-confidence. They encouraged me and made me believe that I could be and do whatever I chose in life.

Mother knew how much I loved to ice skate. She took this photo of me and wrote on the back: *"Es María. Patina en la nieve. Pues, ella quiere ser otra Sonja Henie, la patinadora. Patina muy bien … como ella."*

(It's *María*. She's skating in the snow. Well, she wants to be another Sonja Henie, the ice skater. She skates very well … like her.)

That winter I was going to be the next Sonja Henie.

No question about that.

Mother said I could if I wanted to.

U.S. WAR SAVINGS BONDS

My parents were very patriotic. Father wasn't a U.S. citizen but nevertheless he tried to enlist in the army. He was very disappointed when he was rejected.

1942—The elementary school I attended was having a War Bond rally. The classes were competing to see which class would buy the most U.S. War

Saving Stamps. Each student was given a blank stamp book and Friday was designated as the day to buy the twenty-five cent stamps.

I told my father about the contest and how much I wanted our class to win.

The following Friday as I was leaving for school my father gave me a crisp one hundred dollar bill to buy Savings Bond Stamps. I couldn't wait to get to school ... I knew my class was going to win the contest!

When the teacher called our row, I proudly put the one hundred dollar bill on her desk. I thought her eyes were going to pop out! In 1942 a hundred dollars was a lot of money ... it still is. Such a fuss! The principal was called and I had to go to his office and wait for Father to come to the school.

There was a parent conference and the principal wanted to make sure Father had given me the money. My father became angry. Of course he had given me the hundred dollar bill! How could there be any question about that?

1942—I was in The Memorial Day Parade

THE VICTORY GARDEN

My father hamming it up in our "Victory Garden." This was a program to support the war effort. In the spring the U.S. government sent representatives to various schools encouraging students to plant Victory Gardens. We were asked to sign up and at the end of the summer an inspector evaluated the gardens. Those of us who participated were awarded a special certificate of merit.

I signed up and Father became very much involved. He planted a humongous garden on the side of our house. We had everything: potatoes, corn, squash, tomatoes, red peppers, green peppers, hot peppers, cucumbers, and lettuce.

There was NO way that a child in elementary school could have cultivated that garden. I helped but it was obviously not my project. The inspector came and talked to us and to my utter disbelief; Father said that I had done all of the work! I received the special certificate of merit but even at such a young age I was aware that the inspector knew the garden had been Father's work.

DINOSAURS

"Dinosaurs" was the project assigned to the class. I was seated at the kitchen table going over the outline when Father came home.

He sat down next to me and said, "*¿Necesitas ayuda, querida?*" (Do you need help dear one?)

And with that being said he took me to the hardware store and purchased the materials I needed for my fourth grade project. We sat at the kitchen table working for hours creating dinosaurs out of clay, laughing as we improvised and used rice for their teeth. This was when he was at his best ... we had so much fun!

I wanted the dinosaurs to be standing by a lake and for this scenario to work I needed a waterproof box. Plastic hadn't been invented for everyday use and was not a part of our lives ... that was to come much later, after WW II.

Not to be deterred, he bought a metal container the size of a shoe box and lined it with lead, making it waterproof. We created a shore line with soil, added water to form a lake, arranged an assortment of leaves for the forest and then placed our dinosaurs in the setting to complete the project. It was beautiful!

The day the project was due he drove me to school. I was so proud of what we had created together ... and so was he.

A copy of the original letter Mrs. Shertenlieb wrote to Mother.

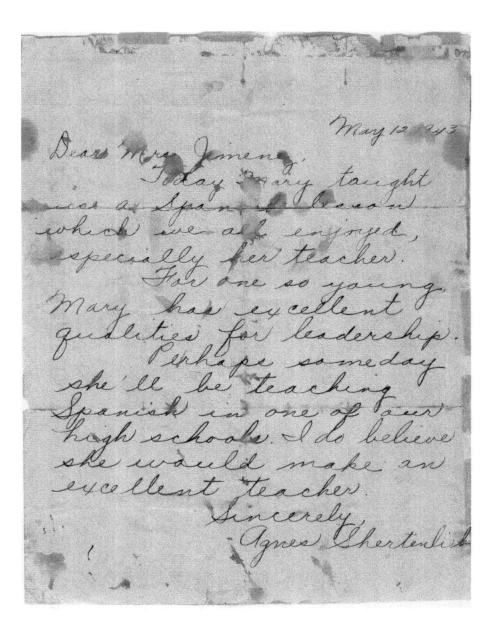

May 12, 1943

Dear Mrs. Jimenez,

Today Mary taught us a Spanish lesson which we all enjoyed, especially her teacher.

For one so young, Mary has excellent qualities for leadership. Perhaps someday she'll be teaching Spanish in one of our high schools. I do believe she would make an excellent teacher.

Sincerely,
Agnes Shertenlieb

June 1948 – Graduation from Island Park Elementary School. I was the Class Secretary and read "The Last Will And Testament." I'm standing 3rd one to the right of our teacher.

1948 – Hanging out in front of Island Park Elementary School before classes begin.

Long Beach

Chapter X

The Lido Beach Hotel, Long Beach, New York faces the Atlantic Ocean and served as a hospital, R&R, and disembarkation point for sailors during WW II. The ordinarily pink hotel was painted gray for the duration of the war to camouflage it from German U-boats that had been sighted in the area. There were submarine lookout towers strategically located along the coastline to protect the community.

Sailors boarded the train at Pennsylvania Station, New York City to get to Long Beach. Island Park was the last stop before the trains crossed a trestle and reached their destination.

The summer of 1942

The sounds of an approaching train and its shrill whistle became Island Park's Pied Piper. I was eight years old and as soon as we heard it my friends and I immediately hurried toward the railroad station and started running alongside the train. At least a dozen or more children waving, cheering and forming V for victory signs with our hands welcoming the sailors home.

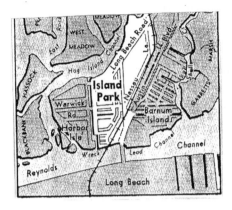

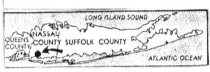

Island Park, New York

They happily responded by tossing their hats to us from the windows. So many hats ... like a flock of white birds flying from the trains.

Thanksgiving of 1943
Mother was preparing dinner when Father appeared with three sailors. Even though it happened sixty-one years ago my memory is clear. As they entered I noticed that one of the sailor's navy blue pants had a big rip at the knee and his shoes were scuffed. He had probably been in a barroom brawl. They all had a strong smell of beer about them, especially my father. They had met at P.J.'s, one of the local bars, and he had invited the servicemen to a home-cooked meal.

Mother was delighted to be able to do something on a personal level for the war effort. "¡*Bienvenidos, están en su casa!*" (Welcome, make yourselves at home!)

She had prepared a delicious meal and they were most appreciative of having been invited for Thanksgiving dinner. Being from the Midwest, it was the first time they had eaten turkey with an assortment of *Puerto Rican* dishes and they told her so.

As they tasted various dishes, "What's this? Tasty! And this? Great!"

They talked about their families, sweethearts and the towns they came from. It was an enjoyable Thanksgiving. I often wondered if they returned home safe and sound after the war. At the time I thought they were older men but they couldn't have been more than eighteen or nineteen years old.

During WW II
The boardwalk was on "blackout alert" for fear of attracting any enemy action. Civilian wardens were assigned to enforce the no lights policy. The photo is Father at one of the darkened concession stands during that time.

After WW II

My family looked forward to long summer evenings, strolling on the board-walk without having to be concerned about the "blackout alert."

It was a perfect outing for relatives and friends; offering a variety of rides, carnival games, concession stands and entertainment. Best of all, as we approached we could see in the distance a panorama of multicolored lights in different shapes and sizes, shining, flashing, and spinning in the night, welcoming us to an evening of fun.

Neighbors

Chapter XI

1940—Celebrating my sixth birthday.

1930—My parents purchased their first home on Newport Road, Island Park, New York.

From the house where I lived as a child you could see a large empty lot between our house and our neighbors. For years both families took great care of the property. They planted trees and shrubs, swings were built for the children, a barbecue and picnic tables completed our own private mini-park. We celebrated the Fourth of July, Memorial Day, and often had joint impromptu summer parties. No one ever questioned who owned the land.

Mother often commented, "*¡Qué buenos vecinos tenemos!* (What good neighbors we have!) *¡Son nuestra familia!* (They're our family!)"

It was true that they were like family but there was no question that our neighbor had a reputation of being dishonest. On more than one occasion he had boasted to my father how he cut corners on jobs and cheated his customers.

1935 – Photo taken before the house was raised. I'm in the carriage in front of our home. **1939** – Father raised the small summer bungalow converting it into a two story residence.

1943 – Photo after the house was raised. The garage is in the background. Our neighbor, Ray and I getting ready to go for a sleigh ride.

He repeatedly encouraged Father to do the same. Mother and his wife were like sisters, making it easier to overlook the neighbor's lack of character.

My parents never thought that he would turn on them. After all as Mother repeatedly said, "*Son nuestra familia!* (They're our family!)"

One day to my father's surprise, the neighbor informed him that he had bought the lot between the two houses. He was willing to sell my parents a few feet for a driveway so that they could have access to the garage from the street.

Father kept saying, "*¡No lo creo! ¡No lo creo!* (I don't believe it!) The bastard bought the land behind my back!"

"*Esperanza*, you know all of my supplies are stored in the garage. If he builds a fence it will be impossible for me to drive to the back of the property!"

Mother always the peace maker, "*¡Cálmate, Ramón!* (Calm down, Ramón!) *¡Estoy segura … todo saldrá bien!* (I'm sure everything will be okay.)"

"*¡No entiendes!* (You don't understand!) Every day I'll have to park my truck in the street and move my material by wheelbarrow from the garage to the truck. It's more work for me! *¡Esto es una locura!* (This is madness!)"

Happy Memories of Newport Road...

My 2nd Birthday

The following evening the neighbor came over to talk business. Father offered him a few drinks in good faith and there was an unopened bottle of liquor on the table as a gift to close the deal.

There was no deal.

Our neighbor, a friend of many years, asked an exorbitant price for a few feet of land. Father refused to pay the sum.

The neighbor smiled and said, "Take it or leave it. But ask yourself, Ray. How are you going to get to your supplies?"

With this said the neighbor informed him that a fence would be put up the next day. As he started to leave he thanked Father for the bottle of liquor.

Father snapped; he grabbed the bottle, told him to get the Hell out and started yelling, "*¡Hijo de Ia gran flauta!* (Dickhead!) *¡Come mierda!* (One who eats shit!) *¡La chingada!* (Fuck!)"

He slammed the door shut almost hitting the man and ended his tirade with the worst possible insults, "*¡Cabrón!* (Cuckold!) *¡Pendejo!* (The nastiest thing you can say to an Hispanic … literally means a pubic hair which is useless.)"

The fence was constructed the next day. After so many good times the families never spoke to each other again. Father decided to move to Marina Road and this time he made sure that the property had a large piece of land on both sides of the house.

2004 – The fence still stands. A car partially parked in the driveway (can't go beyond the chimney), opening the door is very tight. It's impossible for a truck to enter the driveway.

Happy Memories of Newport Road...

1938 – 39 photos of me

Happy Memories of Newport Road...

1937 – My 3rd birthday.

1939 – My fifth birthday.

1935 – My father on the right with friend after a snow storm.

1937 – me on my father's car.

1937 – Mother and me.

Happy Memories of Newport Road…

1935 – My father holding me on the car window.

1935 – Neighbor taking me for a walk.

Happy Memories of Newport Road...

Both photos of me in front of our house.

1939 – Me in front of my house.

1940 – Ray is 1 and I'm pushing the carriage.

1938 – My father standing on his car, neighbor looking on.

Happy Memories of Newport Road...

1943 – Ray's 4th birthday,
Ray is in the middle
with friends.

1942 – Ray's 3rd birthday,
Ray is 1st on left and
I'm 1st top left.

1941 – Me.

1941 – Friends, me 2nd from
the top.

1946:

The dime with Roosevelt's profile, is issued in part commemorating his support for the March of Dimes campaign to

Ex-Lax

Chapter XII

I was twelve years old. Ray was seven. He was incorrigible, always getting into everything, especially if it was mine. I had absolutely no privacy, and forget about hiding anything; he would find it. It was frustrating and infuriating.

I always kept a stash of assorted candies in my bedroom in the top drawer of my bureau. Ray would come into my room and eat them all, leaving a trail of candy wrappers behind and then laugh about it.

While shopping with Mother in the local drug store I saw Ex-Lax on the shelf. It was packaged just like candy.

What a great idea!

I bought it and a chocolate Hershey bar, unwrapped it and replaced it with the Ex-Lax bar. I put it in my candy stash and promptly forgot about it.

It was winter and it had been snowing heavily. Ray wanted to go out and play in the snow. In the 1940s, snowsuits and all winter gear were made of wool. Nylon, polyester, and synthetic clothing would come into our lives only after World War II.

It was snowing, so Mother had to go through the whole routine of dressing Ray to go out and play. It was a chore: sweater, snowsuit, galoshes, gloves, hat and finally ... off he went to play in the backyard.

I was doing my homework at the kitchen table, and Mother was cooking. All of a sudden ... we heard these God-awful screams. It was Ray screaming, "*¡Mamá, Mamá, Mamá!*"

We ran to the door.

What could have happened to Ray?

He had on a one piece snow suit with a zipper (I remember vividly; the color was maroon) and it was filled with <u>shit</u>! Mother raced him to the bathroom; stood him in the bathtub and undressed him. She showered him down as quickly as possible and seated him on the toilet. He stayed there for a couple of hours. He had diarrhea. There was no way of stopping it. The smell in the bathroom was awful! Mother had her work cut out for her soaking, washing, and rinsing everything he had been wearing.

I felt sorry for him but there was nothing I could do so I went back to the kitchen and continued doing my homework. Mother was frantic and started asking Ray questions.

She was like the grand inquisitor; once she started investigating something, she was relentless. She was like a bulldog with a bone. We used to call her the *Puerto Rican* Sherlock Holmes.

"*¿Dónde estabas?* (Where were you?) *¿Con quién estabas?* (Who were you with?)" Ray was yelling, "Speak English! Speak English!"

At a very young age Ray had adamantly refused to speak Spanish and he would throw a tantrum if anyone spoke to him in Spanish. He didn't want to be different from his friends.

Mother: "*¡Está bien, está bien entonces hablamos en inglés!* (Okay, okay then we'll speak English!)"

"What did you eat?" When she asked him that question my blood suddenly ran cold. I never thought anything like this would happen.

The Ex-Lax! Oh my God! Ray ate the Ex-Lax! I was dead! She would kill me!

My only hope was that she wouldn't figure it out. Fat chance of that happening. I knew she would get to the bottom of it. Talk, talk, talk … blah, blah, blah … You had candy? What kind of candy? Where did you get the candy? Maria's room?

Mother: "*¡María!*"

A time of concern growing up was when mother closed her mouth tightly so that you could barely see her lips. It gave the appearance of a straight line across the bottom of her face where her mouth should be. This was always accompanied by the sound, "Mmmmm, Mmmmm, Mmmmm." The facial expression combined with the sound meant one of two things. They were thinking lips … this was good because she was mentally problem solving … or, they were punitive lips and you were in trouble.

She called again … louder this time, "*¡María,* Mmmmm, Mmmmm, Mmmmm!" She was standing in front of me with her arms crossed … they were definitely not thinking lips.

That was it. I broke down and confessed. I felt terrible; how was I supposed to know that Ray would eat the whole bar of Ex-Lax and get so sick? I didn't think there would be such traumatic results.

"*¡Pero María, cómo se te ocurre hacer algo así a Ramoncito?*" (But *María*, how could you think of doing something like that to Ramoncito?)

"*¡Dios mío! ¡Es posible que se muera!*" (My God! It's possible, he could die!)

I kept saying, "*¡Lo siento, lo siento! ¡Palabra mamá, no sabía que eso iba a pasar!* (I'm sorry, I'm sorry! My word Mother, I didn't know that that was going to happen!)"

Mother had strong hands and when you were smacked you felt it but good! I was dead. Today it would be considered child abuse, no question about that.

One good thing did come out of the scary incident. Ray never went into my candy stash again. For years whenever we got together he brought up the Ex-Lax incident. He never forgot it!

La Marqueta

Chapter XIII

To my dismay, my father's favorite barbecue was *lechón asado* (roast suckling pig). He would dig a barbecue pit in our backyard and invite the neighbors over for a "Mexican picnic."

1940s

Father loved barbecuing! It was a big occasion at our house. We had to make a special day trip to Spanish Harlem to *"La Marqueta"* (The Market) to buy groceries for the occasion. Items like *bacalao* (cod fish), avocados, *plátanos* (plantains), and *lechón asado* (roast suckling pig), were unavailable locally.

"La Marqueta" was located under the Fifth Avenue L in Spanish Harlem. It was blocks long and when you opened the doors, you were overcome by all kinds of different aromas associated with the tropics.

"La Marqueta" —had the sweet pungent smell of ripe pineapples and sugar cane. That strong salty fish smell of *bacalao* (dried cod fish). *Bacalao* smelled so nasty that Mother kept a slab of it nailed to the wall in the garage. (Mother would always tell us that if we didn't bathe properly we would smell like *bacalao*, a fate worse than death!) When she needed *bacalao* she would cut a piece from the slab and bring it into the house to cook. As bad as *bacalao*

smelled, it was absolutely delicious when it was prepared in a salad with slices of onions, avocados, olive oil, and vinegar or better still, when Mother made *bacalaitos fritos* (this was shredded cod fish mixed in a seasoned batter and deep fried in oil).

"*La Marqueta*" —had the delicious aromas of chickens, ribs, and roast pigs (marinated in wonderful spices) cooking on spits.

"*La Marqueta*" —had the sweet smells of *dulce de coco* (coconut candy) and piraguas (*Puerto Rican* snow cones) with all kinds of wonderful flavored syrups, coconut, *tamarindo* (tamarind), *fresa* (strawberry), and *mango*.

My parents loved spending a good part of the day shopping there. "*La Marqueta*" had everything that you couldn't find in Island Park. You could even buy clothing. It was as if you had been magically transported to *Puerto Rico*.

Afterwards we would go to a Spanish restaurant and then to a Spanish movie.

Father especially liked the Mexican movies featuring *Cantinflas* (a famous Mexican comedian). They were in their element because they were with Hispanics. They didn't feel like outsiders.

As a teenager I was mortified when Father decided to barbecue. It was the whole procedure of preparing the roast suckling pig and everything that went with it. Of course when the meal was ready to be served, he had to blow a bull's horn to announce that dinner was ready. I died … I didn't want to be different.

How I carried on. Please, why couldn't we have hamburgers and frank-furters like the rest of the families? Why couldn't we have potato salad, cole-slaw, and baked beans instead of *arroz con habichuelas* (rice and beans). Why couldn't we have an American picnic? Our neighbors on the other hand loved it and I had to admit to myself it was delicious.

1940's
Father is hamming it up in the backyard.

Above the clothes line you can just make out
the electric line going into our house. One of
my friends said, "Don't forget to mention in your
book the time your Father made a piñata for your
birthday party. He threw the rope over the electric
line going into your house, and I was afraid to hit
the piñata and get electrocuted."

Father and I are in the backyard.

1936 – I'm with my father, getting ready to drive to New York City to "La Marqueta" to spend the day. He was very proud of his car. The other photo is of me in a small playground in Spanish Harlem.

Spanish Harlem

Chapter XIV

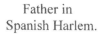
Father in
Spanish Harlem.

October, 1947 I was in the eighth grade in the Island Park Elementary School. My parents were no longer living together. It was a strange arrangement because Father lived downstairs and Mother, Ray, and I lived upstairs. He came upstairs whenever he wanted to. Mother cooked for him and took care of his clothes.

One night we heard some god-awful groans and guttural sounds. Mother and I went downstairs, followed the sounds, and peeked in the kitchen window. Father was seated at the kitchen table eating a big steak and French fries. He would eat, take a sip of wine, and would make horrible sounds. He would pause, laugh, and start all over again.

We didn't know it at the time but he was high on heroin. Later that year we were cleaning the garage and found hundreds of empty vials of heroin. He had thrown them into the rafters after shooting up.

Very often during school nights Father would come home about one in the morning with pizza. We had to get up and eat it. If Mother rejected the pizza an argument would quickly escalate and then there would be no sleeping. This way we ate the pizza, thanked him, and went back to bed. I was thirteen and learning how to survive. To this day I can get up in the middle of the night and go right back to sleep ... I had plenty of practice as a child.

Father would disappear for days. One evening I was downstairs in his apartment and heard his truck pull into the driveway unexpectedly. No one was allowed to be there when he wasn't home. I knew I'd catch hell if he caught me there. It was too late to leave so I hid in the closet. It was early and I thought he would come in to get something and leave. I was wrong. He came in with a friend and they made themselves drinks and sat in the living room. I could hear everything they were saying.

His friend asked, "So, *Ramón* which *puta* (whore) did you like?"

My father laughed, "*¡Pues, me gustó la coja!* (Well, I liked the cripple.) You know she tries harder to please because she's crippled."

His friend laughing, "I never would have guessed that! I think I'll ask for her the next time!"

Oh my God! Please have them leave! I don't want to hear this!

It seemed like an eternity before they finished their drinks and talk about the brothel they'd just come from. It was an education about the seamy side of life and I was hearing it from Father. They finally left. I felt sick. I could never look at him again in the same way. He disgusted me. I never told anyone about what I had heard. I felt so badly for Mother. Every time she did or said something nice for Father, I felt like smacking him.

Mother had three java birds that she kept in a birdcage in the kitchen. One afternoon we found the birds dead. Father, high on heroin, had drowned them under the kitchen faucet and lined them neatly in a row on a paper towel on the sideboard of the kitchen sink. We were devastated, scared and at a loss as to what to do.

It was the last straw. She made a few phone calls and that night we packed and moved into the city. She had a friend in Spanish Harlem who

I loved riding my bike ... Island Park was a wonderful town in which to grow up !

had offered us a place to stay. It wasn't much but she had an extra bedroom in the apartment. Ray and I had no idea where we were going. It happened so fast. I remember the neighborhood was raucous, noisy, and was located near the Fifth Avenue El.

After living in Island Park the city was like being in a foreign country. In Island Park we walked to the beach with our friends. We were relatively safe to come and go as we pleased, as long as we were home in time for dinner. In Spanish Harlem, we weren't allowed to go out alone. It was as if something bad was expected to happen. The city was loud, unfamiliar and very frightening to Ray and me.

The first night was a night from hell. We were exhausted mentally and physically and fell asleep immediately. All of a sudden I felt something crawling over me! I screamed and we turned the lights on. Oh, my God! There were cockroaches all over the bed! It was frenetic, the three of us getting rid of them. We slept with the lights on ... they only came out if the lights were turned off. There was no way of controlling the cockroaches.

There were neighbors, above you, under you, and on either side of you. If one person had cockroaches, everyone had them. The three of us fell asleep holding each other and crying. Mother was an immaculate homemaker and Ray and I were always clean and well dressed. This was hard for her to take.

She enrolled us in school the next day. It was totally different from Island Park. The apartment was in a very tough neighborhood. I missed Island Park and my friends. I didn't want to be in the city. I had only been there one night and hated it. I wanted to go home.

The second night Father came looking for us. Ray and I were in the bedroom but we heard him begging Mother to come back. He was going to change. Things would be better between them. Mother was adamant, she was not going back. He kept begging and it seemed as if she relented a little. She told him she would have to think about it. He could sleep on the living room couch and she would give him her answer in the morning. She said goodnight and came into our bedroom.

I couldn't believe what happened next! No sooner did mother come into the bedroom and close the door, she put her finger over her lips. She made a soft shhhhh sound. And then out came our suitcases and we were packed and ready to go home within five minutes. She left Father in the living room that night letting him think that she wasn't sure what her decision would be in the morning. All the time she knew very well that there was no way that we were going to stay in Spanish Harlem! No way!

I knew the reason Mother was going back to Father was because of Ray and me. She was going back so that we could have a good, safe lifestyle growing up. She knew she couldn't give that to us in the city. Ray was of special concern, there was no doubt in her mind that he would fall in with the wrong crowd.

The last night in that apartment was a wake-up call for me. I decided that whatever happened I was going to do my damnedest to be independent. I wasn't going to be in Mother's situation and that meant getting an education. It all came together, all the years that she had pushed the importance of schooling. She knew that it was synonymous with independence and she always wanted the best for me.

Father drove us home in the morning. As we approached Island Park, I can't ever remember being so happy. It felt great to be home. The next day I went to school and my friends came running up to me, wanting to know where I had been the past few days. They missed me. I made up some excuse.

If I told you, you wouldn't believe it! It was a nightmare!

My father didn't change. It was true that we lived out of harm's way in Island Park however we were very much in danger within our own home.

For me a safe haven was school. With this realization I became very much involved in school activities and excelled. In my senior high school yearbook "Spindrift—1952." I was chosen "Done Most For O.H.S." In my biography I was described as Oceanside's glamour girl. Mother was proudest of the first as a real accomplishment, not the glamour part. In her eyes that was temporary.

Mary Jiminez Oceanside's glamour girl, Mary has a cover girl complexion...Neat as a pin...Loves dill pickles...Her future holds plans to be an airline hostess. G.O. Council 2 (Vice-pres., Sec.) Bowling 1, Tennis 1, Archery 1, Sportnite 2, Sophomore Class Treasus.

Done Most for O.H.S.
Mary Jiminez   Albert Barr

(My first name was anglicized all through school, Mary instead of *María*. My last name was often misspelled, note my yearbook, *Jiminez*, correct spelling, Jiménez.)

I was married at eighteen and had the first of my three children at twenty. Although married with a family the years that followed saw me working toward getting a degree in education. Mother was so proud when in 1972 I received my degree to teach Spanish (Magna Cum Laude). I know that Mrs. Shertenlieb would have been proud too. In 1943 I was fortunate to have her as my elementary school teacher. Once a week she encouraged me teach a Spanish lesson to the class. I was nine years old. A teacher can make a difference in a child's life. I became a Spanish teacher because Agnes Shertenlieb cared and took a personal interest in me.

1948—Father is on top of his car in different poses. He had just returned from one of his usual four or five day absences. The car is in the driveway and to the left you can see the entrance to his downstairs apartment. Mother, Ray, and I lived upstairs.

Harbor Isle

Chapter XV

1948—There were very few homes on Harbor Isle.

The clam-diggers and fishermen that lived there were without electricity and lived in shacks built over the water. It was a desolate place with nothing but marshland. Fifty-six years later where the shacks once stood, homes now sell for $1.3 million dollars.

Island Park had an Elementary School but students had to travel by bus to Oceanside High School to attend grades nine through twelve. Father was overly concerned about my starting ninth grade and taking the school bus every day. He became obsessed about my well-being. One afternoon he drove me to Harbor Isle.

"Mira, esto es para tí. (Look, this is for you.)" He showed me a small pearl handled gun that he had in his pocket.

I started to cry, *"¡De ninguna manera!* (No way!)"

He was shooting at pieces of driftwood in the tall weeds and wanted me to shoot. *"¡No tenga miedo! ¡Es fácil!* (Don't be afraid! It's easy!) Keep it in your pocketbook in case anyone bothers you.

My father has gone mad!

I didn't want anything to do with the gun and told him so. Before we left to go home he made me promise that the gun was our *secret*. He didn't want Mother to know.

Life got progressively worse. I started dating and whenever he knew that I was going out; he followed me and on more than one occasion threatened my date with bodily harm with the gun that he now carried all the time. I don't know how anyone had the guts to ask me out. It became an ongoing joke; if you date *María* watch out for Mr. *Jiménez*. I was fortunate to have good friends that would look out for me. If I was out on a date and my father showed up; they'd run to tell me so that I could hide from him.

I was popular and very much involved in school activities, I never told him when I was going to participate in any event. He would invariably find out and show up. On one occasion while I was making a speech in the auditorium he appeared out of nowhere, in his work clothes, walking down the aisle, yelling, "*¡Es mi hija! ¡Es mi hija!* (That's my daughter!)" He was escorted out of the building.

My high school years became a living hell.

This was the turning point in which my father descended into his own living hell. We didn't know he was heavily into heroin and alcohol until after his death. His personality changed radically from one minute to the next. He could be perfectly happy and suddenly without warning he would turn on you and work himself into a screaming frenzy. He started talking to himself; who knows what demons he was fighting within his inner being.

My family was trapped on a roller coaster ride that did not end until his violent death on September 26th, 1951, the beginning of my senior year.

RUPPERT **FOR THAT** *SMILE OF PLEASURE*

This is the last known photo of my father taken at P.J.'s, a local pub in Island Park. The beer company took the photo and liked it so much that they wanted to use it to advertise that "Smile of Pleasure."

September 1951 – Father with Mother and Ray.

A Challenge

Chapter XVI

June 1950—I was the recipient of a prestigious award sponsored by the American Legion when I was a junior in Oceanside High School. "Girl's Week" was designed for students to become better informed about government and politics in the United States. One girl was chosen from each high school throughout New York State to spend a week at Skidmore College. The selection was based on the student's grades and involvement in school government. It turned out to be a wonderful experience, offering me the opportunity to meet and spend time with a diverse group of teenagers. Mother was very proud that I had been chosen to attend.

I heard her on the phone, "*¡Sí, por supuesto ... es muy importante y un gran honor!* (Yes, of course ... it's *very* important and a great honor!)"

Mother and I were going shopping.

September 1950—Upon my return, the American Legion made arrangements for my presentation informing the community how 1 had benefited from "Girl's Week." Preparing the speech was not a problem and I had a new outfit to wear but when I was told that it was going to be held in a large banquet hall ... I panicked.

I can't do this!

The thought of the formal table setting threw me off. I started to carry on to Mother, "*¡No sé que hacer!* (I don't know what to do!)"

Mother was exasperated, "*¡María con calma! ¿Qué pasa?* (Maria calm down. What's the matter?)"

"*¡No entiendes!* (You don't understand!)"

"*¡Pues, dígame!* (Well, tell me.)"

I explained that I didn't know which fork, knife, or spoon to use. There was too much silverware on the table at a banquet place setting. I'd make a fool of myself. I wasn't going.

Mother's response was: I was going, and that was that. We simply had to research the existing problem. Her first thought was to go to the library and review the books that had photos of table settings. It sounded like a good plan until we started going through books and came across countless pages of place settings. It was impossible to memorize them all.

She sat me down, held my hands and said, "*María, por favor* (please) just look and see what everyone else is doing. Take a sip of water, pick up your dinner napkin, say a few words to the person sitting next to you and notice which knife or fork everyone is using. *No hay problema* (There s no problem.) Remember … *¡Adelante!*"

What a relief it was for me now that I had a plan of action. I went to my first formal banquet and had a great time.

To this day if I'm not sure which utensil to use, I pause and make a mental note of what everyone else is using. When I do, I smile to myself and think of Mother.

I can hear her saying, "*¡Adelante, María!*" No matter what the challenge, there was never going backward or hesitating … only, "Forward, *María!*"

1950: *The Korean war began.*
The comic strip "Peanuts," created by Charles M. Schulz, was first published in nine newspapers.

The Door Closed

Chapter XVII

The door closed.

"*¡Carajo!* (coll. Shit! Hell!) *¡La Chingada!* (Fuck!) *¡Come mierda!* (One who eats shit!)"

We knew it was Father muttering to himself, and for him to be home so early was not good. This meant that he'd been drinking and was in a foul mood. Years later we learned that he had been a heroin addict, a mainliner, which accounted for his bizarre behavior. At the time we thought he was just an alcoholic … but in reality he had been heavily into booze, gambling, and drugs. It was as if he were hell-bent on putting himself into an early grave. He had worked so hard to achieve "The American Dream" and then chose to throw it away, while Mother had held on to her dream tenaciously despite the utter chaos in her life. He would die alone … a violent death within the year at the age of forty-seven in Greensboro, North Carolina, en route to *México* by bus.

My brother Ray and I were in our house in Island Park alone that day, when I was sixteen and he was eleven. It was about three thirty in the afternoon and we had just come home from school. Mother wasn't expected until five.

As soon as we heard Father we ran into my bedroom and slammed the door shut. None of the doors had locks and my bedroom had two entrances. Father started yelling and pounding the door with his fists, clamoring for us to open the door. This wasn't possible. We knew that we had to wait it out until five when Mother would arrive and everything would be okay.

Father continued his tirade, "*¡Abran la chingada puerta!*" (Open the fucking door!) "*¡Ahora mismo! ¿Me oyen?*" (Right now! Do you hear me?)

Father was never physically abusive to me or to Mother but he was sadistic to Ray, constantly testing Ray's manhood. He made him kneel with his arms stretched out, palms up, and put books on his outstretched hands one at a time. When the books became so heavy that Ray dropped them, Father would whack him on the head with a book. Then it would start all over again.

Father would say, "*¡Ahora veremos quién es el verdadero Macho.*" (Now we'll see who the real Man is!)

It was a cruel game at Ray's expense, as was forcing Ray to sit in a dark closet. Other times he took Ray for a ride in his truck, made him get out miles from home, and walk back by himself.

Neither Ray nor I by ourselves could hold the door shut while he tried to push his way into my room. It took the strength of us both to keep the door closed. When he failed to force the door open it suddenly became very, very quiet. Was he silently making his way to the other door to burst in on us? The moment we heard a noise we ran to that door. He never broke in when we were together.

What stands out most vividly in my mind is that while we were both holding that door closed, Ray and I could hear and feel each other's hearts pounding with fear. I'll never forget that horrible feeling, or forget the sound of our hearts. We were as one being.

Whenever I see Ray and something comes up pertaining to a family crisis, he always looks at me and says with a sad smile, "It takes two to hold a door closed, right, *María*?" Immediately we connect as if a bolt of lightning hit us simultaneously. It's something that we share that no one can ever come close to understanding.

Ray was twelve years old when Father passed away. He never shed a tear.

Shattered Lives

Chapter XVIII

It was September of my senior year at Oceanside High School. It was going to be a great year! I was looking forward to Homecoming, General Organization activities, the Senior Prom, and of course selecting a college.

No one else was home when a knock sounded on the front door. Opening the door, I saw two men standing, waiting patiently. They could have been models in the Sunday New York Times Magazine Section. They were tall, impeccably dressed in camel coats, gloves, and expensive shoes. Fedora hats completed their outfits.

"Does Raymond Jimenaise live here?" (I was used to our name being mispronounced.)

"Yes, can I help you?

"Is he home?"

"No, he's my father. Can I give him a message?"

"When do you expect him home?"

"I don't know. What's your name so I can tell him who stopped by?"

"That's okay, he'll know what it's about."

They left. Although they were polite, they made me feel uneasy. That evening I told Father about the men. He blanched and left without saying a word. He didn't return that night. The next day Mother and Ray left early. I was getting ready to leave for school when I heard Father's truck in the driveway. He came in and told me that he was leaving; he was going back to *México*. It would be his first time back since he left in 1920. When he said he was leaving he meant, **now** ... this very minute.

I didn't understand what was going on. He just kept repeating that he was leaving and wanted me to go with him. Mother and Ray were to be left behind. We didn't have time to pack. Whatever we needed we would buy later. His plan was to travel by bus from the Port Authority Terminal in Manhattan to Texas and from there to *México*.

He was desperate and started yelling. The argument escalated. At seventeen I was quarrelling with my father about adult issues. I hated it. All the years of dysfunction and abuse came to a head. I wanted to be thinking about school, dating, the prom, anything but this!

The men had come to the house to collect money. My father was over his head in debt for gambling and drugs. He had no choice but to leave or face their wrath. They meant business.

The fighting was nonstop. We said horrible things to each other that I regret to this day. They still haunt me.

"*María*, you don't understand. I have to leave! They're looking for me!"

"Why? Why are they looking for you?"

"*María*, come with me! Look, I have lots of money!" He showed me a money belt stuffed with hundred dollar bills.

"What about Mother and Ray?"

"I'll send for them later! Come with me, we'll have a great life there!"

"How can you think of leaving them? Get out! Go!"

"*María, te ruego, ven conmigo!*" (*María*, I'm begging you, come with me!)

"*¡Jamás!* (Never.) Go to your wonderful *México*! I don't care! We'll be better off without you! I hope you never reach *México*!"

He left. I was the last one in the family to see him alive.

Three days later the FBI came to my high school. They told me that Father was dead. I was escorted to their car and was taken aback to find that my brother had already been told. Ray was in the back seat of the car. He looked so little and alone. We left with them to pick up Mother at her job. Ray and I waited in the car while they went and told her the bad news. I can still see her coming down the stairs of the building, holding on to the railing crying. She got into the back seat sobbing and gathered us into her arms; holding us as close as she could. I could hardly breathe.

It was the FBI that notified us because Father had died out of state, and it was under their jurisdiction to inform the next of kin. To this day I resent the way the FBI handled the matter. First, from their office in Long Beach they went to the Island Park Elementary School, where they picked up Ray, twelve years old. Then they drove to the Oceanside High School to pick me up. The last stop was Freeport, where Mother worked. The route they chose was convenient for *them*.

Wouldn't it have been more humane if the FBI had broken the news to Mother first, and then picked me up with Mother as support? Ray should have been picked up last with Mother and me already in the car. I know that it was handled in this insensitive, callous way because we didn't matter. We weren't a prominent family. It was 1951 and the FBI was all-powerful. Our name was *Jiménez* and we were Hispanic.

The shock of his death was just the first wave; what followed was worse. Mother was told that she had to go to Greensboro, North Carolina, to claim his body. We later found out that it wasn't necessary for us to go. Mother and I took the same route Father had taken by bus. It was hell for me. I kept thinking of the argument we had had the day before and the hateful things we had said. I wished him dead and my wish had come true. (I never told Mother about the argument.) What was he thinking as he took the same trip?

He ran out of drugs on the bus, became violent, and was thrown off the bus in the middle of nowhere. He was picked up by the local police and taken to a nearby hospital because he was incoherent. Father had a heart attack related to drug withdrawal and died alone.

As soon as we arrived in Greensboro we went to the sheriff's office. Within a few minutes Mother signed papers and was given his personal effects.

I looked at his belongings. *Where is the money belt stuffed with hundred dollar bills? Why is his wallet empty?*

The sheriff offered his condolences. He looked at Mother and said, "Your husband died calling for you. He died calling for *María*."

Mother looked at me and then at the sheriff. She replied softly, "That's my daughter's name."

It was an awkward moment. Mother and I never talked about what the sheriff had said but I know it hurt her. I was on Father's confused mind because I was the last one he had seen and fought with.

In the days that followed I felt as if I was living a nightmare. Father was dead ... and I had wished him dead and meant it at the time.

The funeral arrangements and all that entailed without the support of a family was very hard on all of us. Mother put up a strong front for Ray and me, but inwardly she must have been terrified. She had no family and was totally alone with two children.

Catapulted into adulthood, there I was, seventeen years old, picking out a casket and clothes for my father to be buried in.

Oh God .... please help us! This is a bad dream; let me wake up from this nightmare! Papá, forgive me ... I didn't mean the things I said to you!

Mother now considered me an adult and allowed me to spend hours at Tower's Funeral Home, alone with my father. She was distraught ... her world was falling apart. The funeral was just the beginning of what she would have to face by herself. How was she going to manage financially without him?

I sat in the funeral home, afraid to look at my father. I just sat and looked at the casket from afar. As time passed, little by little I approached the coffin until I was right next to it. I looked at his face. He seemed at peace, so quiet. It was strange. I had never seen him this way. He was always animated and full of life, never quiet. I found myself talking to him and to a degree that calmed me. I kissed him on the cheek to say a final goodbye. I was struck by the cold, marble-like touch of his skin.

¡Perdóname, Perdóname ... te quiero! Adiós, hasta otro tiempo. (Forgive, me, Forgive me ... I love you! Goodbye until another time.)

The funeral service at the Catholic Church in Island Park did not comfort me. Years prior to his death Father had made some scathing remarks to the priest. Among other things, *"Ustedes son payasos! ¡No son verdaderos hombres!"* (You're all clowns! You're not real men!) Because a close relative of his in *México* had been raped by a priest, he always felt contempt toward the clergy. At the funeral service the priest didn't have one kind word to say about my father.

Throughout the service he kept saying, "Repent! Repent! Repent!" At one point I visualized Father suddenly sitting up and screaming, "I Repent!" I walked out before the service was over.

I don't know how, but life went on. My senior year was a blur. With no life insurance, the only assets Mother had were a two-family house and a car. She worked in a coat factory in Freeport to make ends meet. I never knew anyone who could save money like Mother. She always kept five one-hundred-dollar bills tucked under the linoleum in the corner of her bedroom in case of an emergency.

There were a lot of expenses. Mother went to the Welfare Office to see if she could arrange some kind of a loan to tide us over. She came home and was very angry and upset with the system.

"¡No puedo creerlo!" (I can't believe it!)

"They can't give me a loan but if I sign over the house and car they'll give me money without having to pay it back! There's no way I'm giving up my home and car! We'll manage." And manage we did.

College was out of the question. June was rapidly approaching and everyone was making plans for September except me. There were no scholarships or student loans available at that time. For my yearbook biography they asked about my plans after graduation. I knew I wasn't going to college. I just said the first thing that came to mind ... an airline hostess.

My plan was to get a job locally in Island Park or Long Beach and help out at home. Mother would have none of that. Under no circumstances would she have me work locally. She had already formulated a plan of action and needed my guidance counselor's input to implement it.

My guidance counselor discussed what our options were. Mother made our financial situation clear from the start. I had good grades, had always been very active in school and it was expected that I would go to college. They figured out that I could attend the Latin American Institute located on Fifth Avenue near the Fifth Avenue Library in Manhattan. I would become a bilingual secretary. Mother saw it as a beginning and I was ecstatic. I never thought I'd be able to continue my education so soon.

I went to the prom, graduated from Oceanside High School in June of 1952 and immediately started my studies at the Latin American Institute in July of 1952.

Working part time in the Famous Fashion Shops in Penn Station covered my train fare, books, and lunches. Ray worked in a bowling alley after school. Mother renovated the downstairs and rented it year round. There was also a bungalow in the back that she rented for the summer months. It seemed as if all we did at the beginning of the summer of 1952 was paint!

"*¡Adelante, María! ¡Todo saldrá bien! ¡Tienes que tener fé!*" (Forward, Maria! Everything will be okay! You have to have faith!)

She was right, but it took years for me to come to terms with myself about the last time I saw Father alive. Mother's words and her spirit have helped and sustained me during the hard times of my life.

Summer '52 – Me at home & Long Beach.

JUNE 1952 –
The Senior Prom

July 1952 –
Latin American Institute

1958—*The first transatlantic passenger jetliner service was begun by British Overseas Airways Corp. with flights between London and New York.*

Brother Ray

Chapter XIX

"Showing off. Always, Ray"

March 1958—Ray enlisted in the Marines and wrote on the back of this photo. "Real crazy, Eh. Love always, your brother Ray."

My brother Ray is a Damon Runyon character.

Ray has never done anything in a conventional way. As a child on more than one occasion he forged Mother's signature excusing himself from school. While in Marine Corps boot camp he was often ordered to sleep in a garbage truck for repeatedly disobeying orders. Always the rebel and with good reason; our Father abused Ray both mentally and physically as a child on a consistent basis. The effects scarred him for life.

Ray was in his thirties and still afraid to go to bed at night. He felt our Father's ghost was in the closet waiting to taunt him.

Finally summing up enough courage to confront his fears, he jumped out of bed, flung the closet door open and screamed, "Come out of there, you son of a bitch! I'm not afraid of you anymore!"

No one was there. He had put that dreaded fear to rest forever.

At our Father's funeral he said, "Your Father is dead but I still have Mother."

He is handsome, a charmer (women have always been attracted to him), smart, a hard worker, has a great sense of humor, a vicious temper, and is totally unpredictable. There is a very dark side to him. You can't count on him, but when you least expect it he's there for you.

As children I was Father's favorite and Ray was Mother's favorite. It was a reality. I never understood the dynamics of our family and how this evolved but it didn't mean that we weren't loved by the other parent.

I excelled in school and Ray called me the "goody two shoes" of the family who could do no wrong. He always referred to me as "Sister Mary," the nun. He found it difficult to follow in my footsteps, teachers often compared us and he was a poor student. He also hated the regimen of being cooped up in school.

Ray is two years old... with my father.

Wrestling in High School was his opportunity to excel. He won quite a few trophies and was Long Island Champion in his league. I went to one of his meets to be supportive and I couldn't believe what I observed. Moments before the start of the match, the two opponents faced each other, Ray puffed himself up, his entire body became tense, primed to leap forward and attack, the veins in his neck stood out, he made a loud awful grunting sound, and the expression on his face was fearsome. His opponent was taken aback which immediately gave Ray the advantage and he won quickly. There is another side to Ray. When his back is up against the wall he is someone to be with reckoned with.

1958—He dropped out of school and Mother signed papers for him to join the Marine Corps. Ray was the personification of what I envisioned as the ideal marine. However, he lacked the self-discipline that is an integral part of succeeding in the Corps.

I married and we drifted into totally different worlds. We hadn't always gotten along but I have always thought of Ray with a sense of love and sorrow, always remembering the chaos of our shared childhood.

VICIOUS TEMPER

The name *Ramón Jiménez*, is obviously Hispanic. There is no denying that in 1958 there was prejudice that permeated the armed forces.

The first incident happened in the beginning of his enlistment in the Marine Corps. He had gone to the barbershop and the barber did a hack job on his hair by gouging it and cutting it unevenly. Surprisingly, there were no mirrors so Ray couldn't see what the barber was doing. Everyone that was there thought it was funny and they were laughing and making fun of his name.

"You're really going to like this haircut, <u>JIMENAISE!</u>"

Ray had a beautiful head of black wavy hair and took great pride in it. He went back to the barracks, looked in the mirror and couldn't believe what the barber had done. He didn't say a word, took his Marine Corps belt with the thick metal buckle and waited outside the barbershop until everyone left for the evening.

Ray stepped inside, locked the door and windows and beat the barber to a pulp with the belt, "You know what? I really <u>DON'T</u> like this haircut!"

Mother called me, *"Dios Mío, María,* what's a stockade? That's where *Ramoncito* is."

I don't remember how long he was in the stockade but I know no one ever bothered him again. He soon had the reputation of being someone not to mess with because if you made that mistake you'd get it back twofold.

Ray had to go through boot camp twice. The sergeant in charge of his group was a real hard-nosed bastard but Ray respected him tremendously. He learned a lot from him. The sergeant did his job well and made sure that if his men were in combat they would survive.

Ray told me, *"María,* the bastard made me go through boot camp twice but he was fair. I liked the guy. If I ever saw him again I'd shake his hand and thank him."

WARPED SENSE OF HUMOR

During Marine combat maneuvers in *Puerto Rico,* Ray's group had R & R time. The beaches and the beautiful water of the tropics looked inviting. They went swimming while one of the men stood watch to see if any sharks came into the area. He was to signal the men in the water of any imminent danger.

They were swimming when Ray noticed the guard on shore waving frantically, ***shark in the***

area! He didn't say a word to the rest of the men. He started swimming to shore as fast as he could. When he was halfway to shore he started yelling, warning his buddies of the shark sighting. The men were so scared, they started swimming as fast as they could toward shore.

Their adrenalin must have been pumping because not only did they reach shore in record time, but to Ray's amazement they passed him by and he ended up being the last man in the food chain. They lay on the beach exhausted and laughing at Ray. The person laughing the hardest was Ray; the joke was on him and he thought it was funny as hell.

ENTERPRISING

Ray's term of enlistment in the Marine Corps ended and he received severance pay which was a fair amount of money.

One morning Mother called, *"¡Maríia, tu hermano es loco! (María,* your brother is crazy!) He's been home a few days and he's into everything! My garden! My garden! He starts early in the morning and wakes up the neighbors!"

"¡Con calma, Mamá! ¿Qué pasa?" (Calm down, Mother! What's going on?)

Ray always wanted to have his own business. He never had the personality or the temperament to work for someone else. He had received his severance pay from the Marine Corps and without telling anyone bought a backhoe earthmoving machine. It was quite an investment for someone who didn't have a clue as to how to use it.

He decided to practice in Mother's backyard. He dug a humongous hole and then filled it in. This way … that way … learning how to use all of the instruments on the panel. He was a giant version of "Bob The Builder," a children's toy.

His first excavation job was digging out a basement under an old house, shoring up the sides as he dug. It was no easy task and it was dangerous because the walls could have caved in on him at any time. The operation was a success, and from there he acquired other machinery and his business grew.

A SHORT FUSE

Ray was driving and stopped at a red light. A truck driver behind him was in a rush and as soon as the red light turned green he immediately started beeping his horn impatiently. Ray didn't move.

The truck driver became so infuriated that he got out of the truck, ran over to the driver's side of the car and was in his face, yelling and screaming.

Ray realized he was no match for this huge man who had descended upon him but he didn't care. He still didn't move.

The truck driver became enraged, "What the fuck's the matter with you? Are you color blind? Green means <u>GO</u>! Move your god-damned car or are you too stupid? <u>Stupid, Stupid, Stupid!</u>"

Something must have clicked in Ray's brain because he reacted in a flash. His car had automatic windows; he grabbed the man's arm and pulled it into the car as far as he could. It happened so fast that the startled truck driver didn't know what happened. Then Ray hit the automatic button and closed the window. The man's arm was caught up to his armpit and he was stuck.

Ray slid over to the passenger's side and got out of the car. He calmly walked around the car and beat the shit out of the truck driver.

Ray kept saying, "Now, what do you have to say big guy? What are you? <u>Stupid, Stupid, Stupid!</u>"

YOU CAN'T COUNT ON HIM

I received an urgent phone call from a hospital in Nassau County. A *Ramón Jiménez* had been in a barroom brawl and had broken his ankle. It was serious because not only was the ankle broken, but the shattered bone had gone through the skin and they had to perform major surgery immediately. There was a possibility that his walking would be impaired. Ray had designated me as the next of kin. I drove like a madwoman; going through red lights to get to the hospital. When I arrived he was already in the operating room. I waited and prayed that he'd be all right.

One of the nurses from the emergency room spoke to me. She was very kind and reassured me that he would be fine. There was a good team of surgeons working on him. She told me that all the time they were prepping him for the operation he was in a lot of pain and he kept saying, "I can take it! I'm a Marine! I can take it!"

The operation was a success and with therapy he'd be able to walk. The problem was that Ray had an eighteen year old son with a drug problem whom he had been keeping out of trouble. Ray being incapacitated and in the hospital meant that no one was there to watch him. He asked me to help out by taking my nephew into my home until he was discharged from the hospital. Of course I'd help. I was on my Christmas vacation and had the free time but I had no idea what I was letting myself in for.

Ray's instructions were: first, I had to pick up his son at a friend's house. Next, I had to go to Ray's apartment and pick up a large sum of cash to pay his workers. And the last thing I had to do was to get his **HAND GUN** and put it in a safe place until he left the hospital.

Whew! What was I getting into?

I was in my house alone with my nephew who had a serious drug problem. I had a lot of cash and a gun which he knew I had. Ray would be out of the hospital within the week, but until that time I was going to be alone with someone who was a walking time bomb!

Where should I hide the gun?

I hid it in a spot where no one would ever think of looking ... a bag of lawn fertilizer in the garage. When I told Ray where the gun was, he exploded, "You've wrecked the fucking gun! It's damaged in the fertilizer!"

I didn't care. My nephew thought I had hidden it in my bedroom. I didn't really know what he was capable of doing. I had heard horror stories of what people did under the influence of drugs. I also remembered vividly how my father had behaved the last time I saw him.

I sat my nephew down and said, "Look, if you want to walk out and leave, that's okay. That's between you and your father ... but you know his temper. He will find you and there will be consequences. I have the gun in my bedroom and you'll never find it, so don't try. If, when we've gone to bed you decide to come into my bedroom for the gun and money, forget about it. I'm locking the door, and if I see the knob turning during the night, I'm shooting right through the door. Do you understand?"

My nephew looked at me as if I were stark raving mad, "You're crazy!"

I agreed and from then on we never had a problem.

Ray left the hospital with a full leg cast and stayed with me until he was okay to travel. He was in a financial bind because he had been out of work for so long. He borrowed $6,000. Ray and his son left for Florida without leaving a forwarding address.

I haven't heard a word from him in years. I suppose one day there will be a knock on the door and "Brother Ray" will be there. Who knows?

Ray & Me..
1939
&
1992

1946 – Photos of my family …

    Top Photo: Me, Father, Mother and Ray

    Bottom Left Photo: Ray and me, I'm not happy with Ray, he's always tagging along.

    Bottom Right Photo: Me, Mother and Ray doing his usual antics on the side of the photo.

Mother's Next Adventure

Chapter XX

Mother was eighty years old when she passed away on August 23, 1984. Such a strong presence. It is hard to believe she is gone. I still have her telephone number and I know that if I ever need her, all I have to do is call and she'll answer as she had in the past, *"¡Qué tal, mija (mi hija)! ¿Cómo estás querida y la familia, todo va bien?"* (How are you my daughter! How are you my dearest and is everything okay with the family?)

Mother had arthritis of the knees and was a diabetic. She opted to have a knee joint replacement because she could no longer walk. The surgery was a success but her heart couldn't take the trauma of the operation. She died two months later of heart failure.

I was living in West Islip, New York when I got the call to go to Florida. It broke my heart to see her so frail, clinging to life in the hospital. Where was my mother? The Mother I knew growing up?

I kept trying to will her to live, *"¡Adelante mamá, pues adelante mamá no te vayas!"* (Forward, Mother, don't go!) Adelante, as she had so often told me when she was encouraging me to do something.

The morning that she died I was staying at her home in Miami. At 9:30 I became violently ill, throwing up water. I was dizzy, disoriented, and had to lie down. This lasted for about twenty minutes and then it passed. The hospital called at 10:15 to tell me that Mother had passed away at 9:30. It was the same time that I had become so ill. I knew her spirit, soul passed through me to say a last goodbye before she went on to her next adventure. Eventually, a journey we all take.

Ray and I planned the funeral. Just before we walked down the aisle of the church Ray leaned over and grabbed my arm. He said in a low voice, "Now don't start crying like a baby!" Of course I cried and so did he … Mr. *Macho*.

I should have told him that there was no need to mask his grief … it was okay to cry.

After the service we went back to the house. There was a huge bouquet of long stemmed red roses on Mother's night table. They were tightly closed buds when we left that morning. Upon our return the roses were in full bloom. Ray started to cry, "Look, Mother is smiling at us!" My brother does torture me but there are times that I just want to hug and love him to death!

Mother had requested that her remains be cremated and that her ashes be scattered in the ocean off the Florida Keys. She wanted her ashes to flow with the currents to *Vieques, Puerto Rico.*

Ray and I picked out a beautiful urn. He said he had a friend that had a boat in the Florida Keys and that he would take care of the ashes.

It was done. I went back to New York and Ray stayed in Florida.

Two years later he drove to New York for a visit. I just happened to mention Mother's ashes. He gave me an odd look, no eye contact. I said, "Hello … Ray, you did scatter Mother's ashes off the Keys … didn't you?"

There was a long pause. He replied in a low voice, "No."

I yelled: "What? Where are they?"

"I couldn't do it. I couldn't let her go."

"Ray, where are her ashes?'

Another long pause and he responded in a lower voice, "The urn is in the trunk of my car. That's where she's been all this time. I talk to her while I'm driving."

"Two years in the car! You talk to her while you're driving? *Ramón Jiménez, eres loco!* (You're crazy!) Go to the car right now! … Bring them inside!"

We sat on the sofa with Mother's ashes in the urn between us. It was surreal. We held each other, cried, talked a lot and he promised that he would take the ashes back with him and do as she had requested.

As he was leaving to drive back to Florida I said kiddingly, "*¡Ramoncito, tenga cuidado* (be careful) … I'll bet Mother's pissed that you kept her in the trunk of your car for so long!"

A few days later Ray called me from Florida and he seemed disturbed. He had driven to the Keys with his friend and they had gone out as far as they could in a powerboat. It was midday and the sun was exceptionally bright. They turned the boat around facing the shore.

Ray scattered Mother's ashes into the ocean. The reflection of the ashes swirled in the water. The sun's bright rays reflected on the waves. The ashes took on an ominous, shimmering shape. It scared the hell out of him. He thought Mother was angry with him for having waited so long to carry out her wishes. He visualized her rising up out of the ocean like a great genie and saying in a loud voice, "*Ramoncito, ¿Por qué esperaste tanto tiempo para hacer lo que te pedí?*" (Ramoncito, why did you wait so long to do what I asked you to do?)

Ray looked at his friend and yelled, "Hit it! Let's get out of here."

When he told me what had happened we cried and laughed. We both had closure knowing that her ashes were finally free … flowing towards her beloved *Puerto Rico.*

Or are they? One never knows about my brother.

Las Manos De Mamá (Mother's Hands)

Chapter XXI

1938 –
Mother and I are in front of the movie theatre in Spanish Harlem.

Mother's hands were not particularly pretty. Years of hard work had taken their toll. When I think of her hands, myriad images come to mind.

Tus manos eran trabajadoras. (Your hands were hardworking.)

... You cleaned houses, worked in a laundry or a factory for a living.

Tus manos eran suaves. (Your hands were gentle.)

... You brushed, combed and put ribbons in my hair.

Always stressing the importance of having an education, you made sure that Ray and I were well groomed and prepared when we went to school.

1939—My first day of school

Tus manos eran delicadas. (Your hands were delicate.)

... You swept the patio, holding the broom gently; dancing slowly with an imaginary partner; singing softly ... *"Mi Capullito de Alelí"* ... your favorite song.

Tus manos eran poderosass. (Your hands were powerful.)

...You went to the chicken coop, grabbed a chicken by the neck and with a quick flick and a strong jerk broke its neck. Holding it by the neck you plunged it into a waiting pot of boiling water and swiftly plucked its feathers. A knife was never used to split and quarter the chicken...you just pulled it apart with your hands. You had done this so many times, that in no time, the chicken was ready to be cooked.

Tus manos eran musicales. (Your hands were musical.)
...You strummed the strings of a guitar in a carefree moment at the beach.

1932 -
Long Beach, NY

One of my happiest memories is going to the beach with the family. We loved swimming, fishing and clamming. How fortunate we were to live in a community that had a beach within walking distance of our home.

A day at the beach could be Island Park Beach, Long Beach or best of all a day at Jones Beach! Walking from the parking lot through the tunnel to the beach was an adventure in itself. Ray and I always ran through the tunnel yelling as we ran, delighted listening to the echoes. On the boardwalk we could smell the salt air and hear the flags flapping in the wind against the mast before we could actually see them. Closer and closer and then there it was ... the ocean with its pounding surf the expansive beach and sky. How beautiful it was.

Tus manos eran excitantes. (Your hands were excited.)

1972
Cruise Ship

... You gambled and played the slots. Friends would usually come over Friday or Saturday evenings to play cards or bingo. They were happy times ... everyone talking, laughing, drinking, dancing, eating and enjoying themselves.

Tus manos eran hábiles. (Your hands were skillful.)

... You cooked your specialties, *arroz con pollo* (rice and chicken), *habichuelas* (beans), *plátanos maduros* (ripe cooking bananas), *ensalada de bacalao* (codfish condite), *lechón asado* (roast suckling pig), **and *arroz con coco*** (rice/coconut pudding) to the delight of family and friends.

Tus manos eran cómicas. (Your hands were comical.)

As a senior citizen you were in a musical with friends. We applauded your part in the chorus line.

Tus manos eran determinadas. (Your hands were determined.)

... You thumbed through comic books looking at the pictures, figuring out what the words meant. You taught yourself to read English.

Tus manos eran de castigo. (Your hands were punitive.)

... When we did something that made you angry you smacked us. Take the time Frank Sinatra was at the Paramount Theatre. There was no way that I was going to miss his performance! I thought I was so smart cutting school for the day with my boyfriend. We had a strategy. We left home in the morning as if we were going to school and met at the Rockvile Centre Railroad Station. I had planned to sleep at my girlfriend's so that you wouldn't know I was cutting. We sat through three shows and had a great day! You figured it out and my girlfriend caved in and told you our plans. When my boyfriend and I got off the train, there you were with his dad waiting for us. You didn't say a word until we were in the car. "*¡No soporto mentiras!* (I won't tolerate lies!)" Smack! "*¿Entiendes?* (Do you understand?)"

Smack! All the way home you were driving and smacking me at the same time. You were so angry, not so much that I had cut but that I had lied to you. My punishment? The next day I had to tell the principal I cut school.

Tus manos eran cuidadoras. (Your hands were caretakers.)

... You tended your rock garden and took great pride in it. Friends and neighbors stopped by and complimented you on its beauty.

Tus manos eran sobrevivientes. (Your hands were survivors.)

... In the Depression of the 1930s you walked by the side of the railroad tracks and gathered bits of coal that fell from passing locomotives to be used in our stove at home.

Tus manos eran caritativas. (Your hands were charitable.)

... *During the Depression it was not uncommon for strangers down on their luck to knock on our door asking for food. You never turned anyone away who was hungry. There was always a cup of Spanish coffee and bread. If it was later in the day you'd make up a plate of food for them.*

Tus manos eran desesperadas. (Your hands were in despair.)

...My father passed away ... you felt alone and distraught. You cried. I remember you wringing and twisting your handkerchief in grief.

Tus manos eran indignadas. (Your hands were indignant.)

... You couldn't get a loan from Social Services for my father's funeral expenses. You could have gone on welfare by signing your house and car over to them. You came home, hands clenched into fists, determined to make it without their help. *"Adelante, tenemos que ir Adelante ... no hay otro remedio."* (Forward, we have to go Forward ... there's no other way.) And we did go *"Adelante."* You worked two jobs. Ray and I contributed by working after school. He worked in the bowling alley. I worked as a babysitter and at Arnold Constable as a salesgirl. That school year, September 1951 to June 1952 was the toughest time of our lives. At the same time we were closer than we had ever been as a family.

Tus manos eran amorosas. (Your hands were loving and tender.)

... Holding your grandchildren.

Tus manos eran frágiles. (Your hands were frail.)

... In the hospital clinging to life.

But most of all I remember...

Tus manos eran cariñosas. (Your hands were loving.)

... When you held me and told me that you loved me.

Mother and Me

¡Adelante! Mother's Legacy

Chapter XXII

November 11, 2003—A friend teaches at an alternative high school in Brentwood, New York. It is comprised of troubled multi-ethnic students who can't succeed in a regular school setting. They are problematic teenagers who are street-smart, tough, and this is their last chance to get a high school diploma. He was reviewing a chapter on "The American Dream" in his history class and thought they might be interested in reading and discussing a few chapters from "¡Adelante!"

Yes, of course I was interested. It would be great if I could take from my past, reach out and motivate even one student in a positive way. Ultimately it could be Mother's legacy.

I knew the risk I was taking, they would either listen to what I had to say or simply tell me to "fuck off." Nothing had ever daunted Mother's spirit and inner strength … with that in mind I went. I had printed copies of the chapters I wanted to read to the class so that they could follow as I read. It turned out better than I had expected. They were genuinely interested, I had piqued their interest and they asked in depth questions wanting to know more about the people in the biography.

One Hispanic girl in particular impressed me; she is seventeen years old, intelligent, and appears to have the drive to succeed in life. She has a ten-month-old baby girl, attends night school, works part-time, and is presently living in a home for unwed mothers since her own mother threw her out when she refused to have an abortion. During the discussion period she expressed her desire to become a nurse but couldn't afford to attend college. The class ended and I distributed a questionnaire for the students to answer, it was strictly voluntary.

The following is what the Hispanic girl wrote:

1. What was your reaction to ¡Adelante!?

I really liked talking to you. It is going to influence me on moving up faster in life. As you were reading your mother still was alive. Thank you very much.

2. Can you relate to my life?

In a way I can and cannot relate to your story because I've been through a lot in seventeen years. My real father was abusive and back and forth from jail due to drugs just like your father. He's not dead yet but now he has aids and is very unhealthy. I haven't seen him since I was eleven years old. He doesn't know he is a grandfather and I really want to reunite with him. All I know is that he lives in Manhattan. I had a baby young and have been through a lot since then. I was put down mentally and emotionally abused. Well I guess everything gets bad before it gets good. You keep saying make the right choice. Why is it that the right choice is always the hardest?

Once a week I volunteer in Southside Hospital's "Born To Read" program working in the maternity ward with Hispanic patients who don't speak English. We emphasize the importance of reading to your child from the moment they are born and I stress the need for them to learn English. I was at an annual luncheon given by the hospital to show its appreciation to the volunteers and by chance was seated next to the Vice President of Nursing at Southside Hospital, New York. We talked and soon realized that we had a common interest. There is a growing need for nurses fluent in Spanish/English, the hospital has initiated a program that will cover all college expenses and is presently looking for candidates that qualify. Did I know of anyone? The Hispanic girl came to mind immediately and we set up a tentative date for an interview.

I contacted the Hispanic student and she was extremely happy to have the opportunity to make a better life for her daughter and herself. I emphasized the importance of making an overall favorable impression at the interview. She was very excited and said with a big smile, "I know, I know. A nice, simple outfit and ... *No Cleavage!*"

May 12, 2004—The Hispanic student had an interview with Southside Hospital's Vice President of Nursing. She was accepted in the program.

September 15, 2004—The Vice President of Nursing and I visited the South Ocean Middle School, Patchogue to meet with the principal and the Guidance Department. She wants to select candidates in the lower grades to make sure they take the right courses to be better prepared when they graduate in preparation for nursing school.

It was going to be a memoir for my children, grandchildren and great-grandson but *¡Adelante!* has taken on a life of its own. This is becoming my retirement "Adventure" making presentations and using Mother's biography to encourage troubled multi-ethnic students and people in general to make the right choices. Above all *never* give up on your hopes and dreams.

Somewhere in the recesses of my mind I can hear Mother saying, "*¡Adelante, María!*"

UPDATE:

Introduced, read, and discussed excerpts from ¡*Adelante!*

October 2, 2004—Hope Ministries, Port Jefferson, New York.

November 21, 2004—Brentwood Alternative High School, Brentwood, New York.

March 15, 2005—Hope Ministries, Port Jefferson, New York

May 6, 2005—Beta Psi Chapter—Pi State - The Delta Kappa Gamma Society International

June 9, 2005—Nassau County Juvenile Detention Center, Westbury, New York.

August 4, 2005—The Delta Kappa Gamma Society International has invited me to present two workshops at the Northeast Regional Conference, Cleveland Ohio. Name of workshop: ¡*Adelante!* Achieving "The American Dream."

Responses To Questionnaire:

What **was your reaction to my talk?**

My reaction was like wow because it seems to me that it take a lot of heart and braveness to sit into of an audience and speak out a hard crecimiento *(the way of growing up) a toughtway. I felt good. I thing that it terns. I do not really know if you include yore son's but I think it will be a great idea because ass you was reading yore mother still was alive.*

Can you relate to my life?

Yes I thing I can relate with home child abuse with my father to aggressive but I thank you for sharing yore first story with us and to be successful is coming out great.

. . .

What was your reaction to my talk?

I thought it was impressive. And how you survived and got through it. I thought it was interesting. And I really like the beginning of the book. Your doing a very good job and keep on going "Adelante"

Can you relate to my life?

No because my mom had an easier life, but also struggled.

. . .

What was your reaction to my talk?

It was really touching and I really think that you touched every single one of our hearts. The little that you read sounded like a very interested book. It was heart touching and funny.

Can you relate to my life?
I guess I could relate a little I mean I don't think my father was that abusive but he was very tough on my brother, him being the oldest and a male, my father expected a lot from and was hard on him!

. . .

What was your reaction to my talk?
I think it was good and it inspire me to continue with my education because at one point I was not goin to continue with my education but now I am goin to continue my education. And I am proud of you for doing all this for your Self. Thank you for coming.

Can you relate to my life?
Not really

. . .

What was your reaction to my talk?
I think it was very interesting to listen to your life story.

Can you relate to my life?
I can relate to your life a little bit with the father and the verbal abuse with alcohol.

. . .

What was your reaction to my talk?
It made me realize that everyone has their own problem. There is always a way to survive in life. Never give up even if times are at its worst episodes. The book is true and sad but it makes you value your life and family no matter what. I Really like your book so far and I know it's going to be a hit.

Can you relate to my life?
I can relate to your life because I live without my father or mother and I am Struggling a lot to keep my dreams together and I will never give up.

. . .

What was your reaction to my talk?
I really like your speech it really is going to influence me on moving up faster In life. Thank you very much.

Can you relate to my life?

In a way I can and cannot relate to your story because I've been through a lot in 17 years my real father was abusive and back and forth from jail due to drugs to just like your father hes not dead yet but now he has aids and very un healthy. I haven't seen him since I was 11 years old. He doesn't know he is a grandfather and I really want to reunite with him. All I know is that he lives in manhattan. I had a baby young been through alot since then. I was put down mentaly and emotionaly abused well I guess everything gets bad before it gets good.

• • •

What was your reaction to my talk?

My reaction was that it's amazing how even 40 or 50 years ago some of the problems people go through now it happened as well back then. Your talk had me on !AWW! only because not everyone is able to talk or write it about a life like yours and be so comfortable. Can't wait till your book gets published. You are a great woman!

Can you relate to my life?

Well, to be honest, my father was never abusive or alcholic or involved in any Drugs but right now as I write this my father is in jail and I grew up without him. I was 6 when he went to jail and due to this it affected my brother. The only Man in the house ended up messing up and being in jail and out ofjail since he was 16. He is 25 now and in jail. So, I grew up without a male role model and even through my traumatizing childhood I've succeeded in school and I thank my mom for being so strong through everything and being both my mom and father. So, I would say that in a way I can relate to you and I'm 17 now and still going Through rough times and bad childhood memories. So, yeah in some way or Another I do relate to your life.

• • •

Mother's Recipes

Chapter XXIII

Mother loved to cook. Family and friends looked forward to her dinners. I have fond memories of everyone sitting around the table just talking and eating for hours on end.

Sundays, no matter who was there, she would cook a big meal. Mother would get up very early and soon the house was filled with the aroma of her specialties. Usually from 1:00 P.M. on there would be an array of friends stopping by, unannounced. Always as the friends came to the front door, Mother invited them to join us.

"*¡Buen provecho, están en su casa!*" (Enjoy your meal, make yourself at home!)

And of course they did.

Just as my father had loved his "Mexican Picnics" with *lechón asado* (roast suckling pig) ... Mother loved her Sunday dinners. I think it was a throwback to her childhood. In *Puerto Rico "Un Asalto"* (an assault) is an old custom in *Puerto Rico*. A group of family or friends plan a get together. The would be host is totally unaware of the fact that they are going to have a party. The guests plan ahead and each person brings something with them: music, liquor, an assortment of food, and whatever else is necessary. Armed with all the goodies the guests appear unannounced at the host's home. They are welcomed and a great "happening" of family and friends is created.

When Mother retired and moved to Florida a prestigious doctor would stop by for dinner from time to time, unannounced. She had watched him as a child during the summers in Island Park. He never forgot her kindness or her cooking and kept in touch with her. The last time she was in the hospital he was in attendance and stopped by to see her every day. He told the doctors and nurses to take good care of her because she had been so special to him as a boy and he thought of her as his second mother.

One Sunday comes to mind. I hadn't been married very long. We were spending the weekend at Mother's. My husband was a hispanophile, had studied at the University of *Puerto Rico* and was fluent in Spanish. He was of

English descent and came from a very conservative family. There was no way that friends would just drop in for a visit with his family, especially at dinnertime. His family was the antithesis of mine.

There was just Mother, Ray, my husband and I at home. As was customary on Sundays, she got up early and started cooking up a storm.

My husband asked, "Why is *Esperanza* cooking so much? Is she expecting company?"

My response, "Maybe … you'll see."

The four of us sat down to eat around 1:00 and then friends started arriving. Each guest brought something, dessert, wine, salad, a special dish, or an appetizer to add to the meal. Mother would invite them to join us; they took plates that were already stacked and waiting for guests, served themselves, and joined us at the table. This scene was repeated, and before we knew it there were twelve people at the table. Everyone was eating, talking, laughing, and having a good time.

My husband couldn't deal with it. So much talking, laughter, and music in the background. He excused himself from the table and went into the living room. There was a moment of silence at the table and then the conversation resumed. Mother took me aside and asked me if he thought he was too good for her friends. I went into the living room and told him he had to come back to the table because he had insulted Mother. He did and apologized to everyone. As the years passed my husband adapted and looked forward to Mother's Sunday dinners. One never knew what interesting people would show up.

And so … whenever I prepare any of the following recipes, I'm flooded with happy memories of Mother in the kitchen doing what she loved to do most for her family and friends… cook.

¡Buen Provecho!

Adobo
(seasoning for meat)

Mash in mortar:
2 teaspoons salt
1 teaspoon dried oregano
2 cloves of garlic
2 whole black peppercorns
Add to the mixture:
1/2 teaspoon vinegar
1 1/4 teaspoons olive oil

Rub the *Adobo* all over the meat. Cover and refrigerate for several hours. Remove the marinated meat from the refrigerator 30 minutes before cooking.

Mother always had a "pilón" (mortar) as pictured. It is a necessity in the Hispanic kitchen.

Arroz Con Pollo
(Rice And Chicken)

18 pieces of chicken thighs (boneless/skinless)
Marinate in salt, pepper and *Adobo* (I like the Goya all purpose seasoning)
1/4 cup olive oil
3 teaspoons *oregano*
3 teaspoons garlic
1 large onion (I use 1/2 frozen bag)
1/4 cup olive condite chopped + 3 tablespoons of juice
Sauté
Add 3 cups of Uncle Ben's rice
Add almost 1 small can of tomato sauce
Add 5 1/2 cups water
Bring to boil, lower heat and let simmer with cover on
After about 15 minutes stir…
Do not stir more than twice.
Cook on low flame until all the water is gone.
I serve with *habichuelas* (beans…recipe below)
Also serve *Plátanos Maduros* (Ripe Plantains) Mother used to go to all the trouble of peeling and cooking the plantains … I highly recommend Goya's *Plátanos Maduros*. They are delicious and microwaveable. A great time-saver. You can find them in the frozen food department.

• • •

Habichuelas
(Beans)

1/2 lb bacon cubed
1 1/2 bags of frozen onions
Cook bacon in a separate pan until brown, put aside
Sauté onions in a deep pan in 3/4 cup olive oil
When the onions are a light brown add the bacon and bacon fat.
Add
1 tablespoon garlic
3 tablespoons *oregano*
3 small cans of tomato sauce
3 small cans of water
3 cans of kidney beans drained (I like Goya's small red beans)
salt, pepper and *Adobo* to taste
Mix well
Bring to a boil, lower heat and simmer for 20 minutes

Caldo Xochitl
(Mexican Aztec Soup)

This is my favorite soup ... very different and "*delicioso*."

6 cups fresh or canned chicken broth
1 whole chicken breast, split in half
1/4 cup vegetable oil
4 ounces of angel hair pasta
1 ripe, unblemished avocado
2 hot *jalapeños*
Salt and freshly ground pepper

1. Pour the broth into a large saucepan and add the chicken. Cover tightly and simmer until the chicken is cooked and tender, 20 to 30 minutes. Remove the chicken when cool enough to handle, remove the bones and skin. Cut the chicken into bite-size pieces and set aside.
2. Heat the oil in a skillet. Break the angel hair into two inch lengths and cook it in the oil, stirring until golden. Do not burn! Drain the angel hair on paper toweling.
3. Bring the broth to a boil. Add the angel hair. Simmer until the angel hair is tender, 5 to 10 minutes. Add the chicken.
4. Peel and seed the avocado and cut into half-inch cubes. Add the cubes to the soup. Chop the jalapenos removing the seeds and then put them in a blender ... making a puree ... add to the soup. Heat thoroughly and add salt and pepper to taste.

Serve in hot cups
6 to 8 servings
Note: *Jalapeños* are available in jars.. .use with caution. They are very hot!

• • •

Ensalada de Aguacate y Tomate
(Avocado and Tomato Salad)

1 large, ripe avocado, peeled and sliced
olive oil and vinegar
dash of *jalapeño* (very little!)
4 beefsteak tomatoes, sliced
1 medium Spanish onion, sliced thin
Salt and pepper
Combine all of the ingredients in a glass bowl.

Ensalada de Bacalao
(Cod Fish Salad)

1 1/2 lbs. salt cod
1 large potato
1 medium yellow onion
1 avocado
3 hard boiled eggs
1 red pepper
1 tomato
1/4 cup of vinegar
1 cup of olive oil
salt and fresh ground pepper

Soak cod in cold water overnight, rinse, and shred. Boil, peel, and cut potato into cubes.

Peel and cut onion into thin slices. Peel and cut avocado into cubes. Slice eggs. Cut red pepper into slices. Cube tomato.

Combine cod, potato, onion, pepper, tomato and eggs in a serving bowl. Mix oil, vinegar, salt and pepper.

Pour over salad and toss.

Serves 5

•   •   •

Bacalaitos
(Codfish Fritters)

1 lb. codfish fillets
1/2 cup water
2/3 cup flour
1 egg
1 onion, diced
1 tsp. chopped parsley
1/2 tsp. ground garlic

Boil the codfish fillets in water, drain to remove excess salt. Shred the codfish fillets into bits. Blend all of the ingredients together. Use a deep skillet, half-full of cooking oil. Preheat the oil on medium high heat. Ladle the mixture slowly into the hot oil. Remove from the skillet when cooked throughout and the edges begin to curl. Place on paper towels to remove excess oil. Serve while warm.

Tortilla Puertorriqueña
(*Puerto Rican* Omelette)

1 large boiled and peeled potato, cut into small pieces
1 large Spanish onion, chopped
8 eggs, beaten
salt and pepper
3 *chorizos* (I like Goya) cut into thin slices. The oil and the special seasonings in the *chorizo* adds a special taste to the omelette.
1/2 red pepper cut into thin slices
1/2 yellow pepper cut into thin slices
1 tablespoon of olive oil (just enough to moisten the bottom of the frying pan)

Put olive oil in large frying pan (I like to use a Teflon pan—it's easier to control the heat without food sticking). Sautee potatoes, onion, *chorizos*, red pepper and yellow pepper over a low to moderate heat until the potatoes, onions, red pepper, and yellow pepper are a golden brown. Add the eggs and salt and pepper. Cook until the eggs are firm.

4 generous portions
Plátanos maduros on the side, delicious! I buy the frozen Goya brand (it's much easier than starting from scratch and you can't tell the difference.)

• • •

Pernil
(Roast Pork Shoulder)

5 lbs. pork shoulder
6 garlic cloves
1/2 teaspoon black pepper
1 teaspoon *oregano*
1 1/2 tablespoons olive oil
1 1/2 tablespoons vinegar
3 teaspoons salt

Remove the skin and fat from the pork shoulder. Make small cuts over the top of the pork. With a mortar and pestle ... crush garlic, *oregano*, and black pepper. Add olive oil, vinegar, and salt. Mix well.

Spread the mixture over the pork shoulder. Refrigerate the meat for at least 12 hours. Cook in a pre heated *350* degree oven for about 2 1/2 hours or until well done.

Lechón Asado
(Roasted Pig)

One 25 lb. Suckling pig, ready to cook
24 cloves garlic peeled
3 tablespoons whole dried *oregano*
1 tablespoon peppercorns
3/4 cup salt
Crush the above in a *pilón* (mortar)
1/2 cup sour orange juice

Make deep gashes on the neck, the loin, legs, shoulders, and over the ribs. Rub seasoning into the gashes as well as inside and outside the pig. Cover with cheesecloth and set overnight in a cool place to marinate. Barbecue the pig, by passing a pole through its body. A slit is cut just under the tail and the pole goes through it and out the mouth opening.

Tie the front and hind legs very tightly around the pole. Place over an open fire of hot charcoal, resting both ends of the pole on Y posts.

Rotate slowly and baste frequently with *achiote*. Cook about 7 hours or until meat is well done.

• • •

Arroz Con Dulce
(Rice Pudding)

4 cups water
1 teaspoon salt
1 teaspoon cloves
1 tablespoon crushed fresh ginger
1 14 oz. can coconut cream
1 cup regular, uncooked rice
1 cup sugar
1 tablespoon butter
1/2 cup raisins

Soak rice in water for about two hours prior to cooking and drain. Add salt, cloves and ginger to three cups of water in a deep pan. Bring to a boil.

Sieve through a colander to remove remnants of the spices. Bring to a boil once again.

Add the coconut cream, rice, sugar, and butter. Cook covered over medium low heat for twenty minutes. Add raisins and blend in. Continue to cook, uncovered, until the rice has absorbed all the water. Pour into a dish about one inch high and allow to cool. Sprinkle ground cinnamon and shredded coconut on the pudding. Cut into squares.

Photo Section

"Mi Familia"

Chapter XXIV

Mi Familia

1926 – My father's brother
Juan Jiménez

No Date – Juan Jiménez
(note – cigarette butts on the dirt floor)

Mi Familia

No Date – My father's sister,
Erlinda

1939 – My father's brother
E. Jiménez

Mi Familia

No Date – My father (Ramón Jiménez) & his brother (Juan Jíménez).

Mi Familia

No Date – My father's relatives
(unknown)
married six months

No date – My father's cousin
Pedro

Mi Familia

No Date – My Father's relatives (unknown).

1929 – My Father's cousin.

Epilogue

Esperanza Peña Jiménez concludes her biography in her own words. (Excerpts from a letter she wrote me dated January 17, 1962

> *Dearest María,*
> *God willing that when you receive this you are all well. Kisses to the girls. And from me many, many kisses and hugs to all...I wish to see you instead of writing to you.*
>
> *Your mother who truly loves you.*

Postscript

February 25, 2004

Vieques, Puerto Rico

It was a trip that was long over-due; I had never been to *Vieques* before. Visiting Mother's birthplace brought to life many of her stories. Mother and *Vieques* continue to be very much on my mind.

Ferry Schedule

PASAJEROS

lunes a viernes

7:00 AM	Vieques-Fajardo
9:30 AM	Fajardo-Vieques
11:00AM	Vieques-Fajardo
1:00 PM	Fajardo-Vieques
3:00 PM	Vieques-Fajardo
4:30 PM	Fajardo-Vieques

Itinerario de viajes hacia VIEQUES

RESERVACIONES

HORARIO:
8:00 a 11:00 AM/1:00 a 3:00 PM.

Favor de reportarse al terminal, una hora antes de su salida.

Fajardo:	(787)863-0705
	(787)863-0852
	(787)863-3360
	1(800)981-2005
Vieques:	(787)741-4761
	(787)741-0233
Culebra:	(787)742-3161

sábado, domingo
y lunes feriado

7:00 AM	Vieques-Fajardo
9:00 AM	Fajardo-Vieques
1:00 PM	Vieques-Fajardo
3:00 PM	Fajardo-Vieques
4:30 PM	Vieques-Fajardo
6:00 PM	Fajardo-Vieques

* Itinerario sujeto a disponibilidad de tripulaciones y condiciones del tiempo.

Where was she born? Where did she live? What was she like as a child? There are so many unanswered questions. As I boarded the ferry in *Fajardo* to *Vieques* I marveled at the vastness and beauty of the Caribbean. It was ninety-one degrees, the tropical sun felt good and the birds soaring in the warm breeze high above gave me a feeling of well- being.

¿Qué estabas pensando, Mamá? (What were you thinking of Mother?) As you left *Vieques* alone, not knowing what your life would be like in New York.

(February 25, 2004 – Vieques)

The *públicos* (cabs) were waiting as the ferry docked. After hiring one for the day, my first stop was the Catholic church. The priest, Father P. Nelson *López*, went through old records dating from 1840–1946. The ledger was so old that some of the pages were crumbling. There was nothing, leading us to believe that Mother might have been born at home and not registered. Father *López* said not to give up hope and that he would make inquiries. He said a Mass for Mother the following Sunday hoping that perhaps some of the older people in the congregation might remember her.

Catholic Church, Vieques

Inmaculada Concepción

Church Ledger, baptisms (L – Z) 1840 – 1946

Father *López* said Mass for Mother:
Saturday, February 28, 2004
7:00 PM ... *Esperanza Peña* ... by her daughter, *María* Tonkiss

PROGRAMA DE MISAS Año 2004		
MISAS DE COMUNIDAD		**INTENCIÓN DE**
SÁBADO, 28 DE FEBRERO		
5:00 P.M. Sta. María		
5:00 P.M. Pto. R.		
7:00 P.M. Pueblo....................+Richard López		Su esposa Delia, hijos y nietos
	+Amanda Ortiz Pérez	Justino y Alicia
	+Andrea Emeric	Su hija Isabel Ortiz
	+Esperanza Peña	Su hija María Tonkiss
	+Silveria Cirilo	Su hija Felícita
	+Lorenzo Galloway	Su esposa e hijos

The priest suggested that we try the hospital (*Registro Demográfico*) where birth records were kept. Again, no luck.

I don't have photos of Mother or her family in *Vieques*. Mother's family is a mystery. Her life began in Island Park at the age of sixteen.

As an adult, Mother visited *Puerto Rico* but she never returned to *Vieques*.